THE NOVEL AND T

THE NOVEL AND THE PEOPLE

by

RALPH FOX

Preface by Jeremy Hawthorn

LAWRENCE AND WISHART
LONDON

Lawrence and Wishart Ltd
39 Museum Street
London WC1A 1LQ

First published by Lawrence and Wishart in 1937
Reprinted with minor corrections, and a Preface by
Mulk Raj Anand, Cobbett Press, 1944
Reprinted with a Preface by Jack Beeching, Cobbett
Press, 1948

This edition, with a Preface and Select Bibliography
by Jeremy Hawthorn, first published in 1979
Copyright © Lawrence and Wishart, 1979

809 .
33
FOX

Printed and bound in Great Britain at
The Camelot Press Ltd, Southampton

CONTENTS

PREFACE

RALPH FOX was born on 30 March 1900 in Halifax, where his father was general manager of an engineering firm. He was educated at Heath Grammar School, Halifax, and at the age of about sixteen went to Bradford Grammar School to work for a scholarship to Oxford University. Fox refers to his place of birth and upbringing in *The Novel and the People* when arguing against the view that *Wuthering Heights* has to be approached as "pure" poetry, and other memories from his childhood can be detected in his second, posthumously published novel, *This was their Youth*.*

Fox won his scholarship to Magdalen College, Oxford, "the most English and loveliest of colleges", as he describes it in *People of the Steppes*, and his studies there included work on the French eighteenth-century encyclopaedists and on oriental languages. The scientist J. G. Crowther, who was at Bradford Grammar School with Fox, comments upon his undoubted talent for translation and his feel for foreign languages, which was to stand him in good stead in his subsequent travels.

Fox had had some military service by the time he went to university; in *People of the Steppes* he recalls apologizing to a Tolstoyan Socialist for having served in the army, but "since my service, like the traditional baby, was only a little one, it was allowed to pass". In the same work Fox mentions that the device of the 17th Lancers was pencilled on his khaki sun-helmet, and recalls a conversation on army efficiency and discipline in which he told his listeners that

[. . .] even the respectable British army plunders when it is cold. I was in an Australian battalion and they would give us

* For bibliographical details of Fox's work, see p. 165.

no fires in billets in December, so we burned the furniture. We also kept the public houses open by force after hours (*People of the Steppes*, p. 117).

According to J. G. Crowther, Fox became interested in social affairs when at university, and a particular interest in the Russian Revolution and its effects led him to volunteer to work with the relief organization of the Society of Friends (Quakers), which was attempting to alleviate the effects of the famine in the young Soviet Union resulting from the civil war and wars of intervention. His experiences with the Quakers are recounted directly in *People of the Steppes* and indirectly in his first novel, *Storming Heaven*. In the former he accepts, implicitly, the description of him volunteered by a lady fellow-passenger in a train as "an idealist who believes in action." Fox was shortly to become a member of the British Communist Party, so we can say that in a technical, philosophical sense he soon abandoned his idealism, but in the larger sense of a belief in the possibility of bettering the world and its inhabitants, the description is one which can accurately be applied to him up to his death. *People of the Steppes* ends with a first-hand account of part of the trial of the Socialist Revolutionaries in Moscow in 1922, and Fox's summary of the trial gives us an interesting idea of his attitude at the time:

Opposite to one another sat those who had desired the Revolution and those who had talked about it, and in a way it was much more than the process of one political party against another, for fixed for a moment on that theatrical platform in accusers and accused were seen the eternally opposed currents of hatred between the man of action and the mere dreamer, between the man for whom life is art and the man for whom art is life (p. 212).

Not the least of the attractions of Marxism for Fox must have been its stress on action, on praxis, as the means whereby human beings gain a knowledge of the truth. It is also likely that this sympathy for action entered into Fox's preference for the novel rather than for the lyric.

Four years after joining the British Communist Party, in 1930, Fox went again to the Soviet Union, this time to do a two-year stint at the Marx-Engels-Lenin Institute in Moscow, involving work on writings of Marx that had appeared in the *New York Daily Tribune*. At the same time, according to the Marxist historian A. L. Morton, he was engaged in reading that formed the basis of many of his subsequent political writings.

On his return to Britain in 1932, Fox was elected to the Communist Party's Central Committee, and from then until his death his energies were dedicated to political activity, both in his writing and in his other work. We should not assume that Fox saw "political activity" in the narrow sense in which the phrase is all too often used today, however. His deep-rooted humanism is as much apparent in his early *A Defence of Communism* as in his novels or his writing on literature. He was aware, moreover, of the dangers of becoming submerged in day-to-day political struggles, and an interesting review of his in *The Communist* of November 1927, discussing R. P. Dutt's *Socialism and the Living Wage*, warns of the urgent need for the Communist Party to justify itself theoretically after immersion in day-to-day struggles during the first seven years of its existence.

In 1934 Fox was involved in setting up the British section of the Writers' International and was elected to its Executive Committee. The same year Fox and others, including Montagu Slater, Edgell Rickword and Tom Wintringham, were instrumental in founding the highly-influential periodical *Left Review*. A year later, in 1935, Fox was a member of the British delegation to the International Writers' Congress in Paris, where he doubtless gathered some of the material he was to use in *France*

Faces the Future (1936). Some time after this he went to Portugal, probably to collect information on the help Fascist Portugal was giving to the Franco insurgents in Spain. *Portugal Now* (1937) is a record of this visit, and although by no means as substantial a work as, say, *People of the Steppes*, shows how Fox, like Marx, could make use of a sustained ironical mode to assert his humanistic values.

Ann Herbert-Richardson (formerly Fox) says that Fox never worked full-time for the Communist Party; but from the time he returned to Britain from the Soviet Union until his death in Spain he undertook much unpaid work for the *Sunday Worker*, *Daily Worker* and for the Party. During this time he supported himself by freelance journalism and writing, including translation work. This did not ensure him a reliable income, however, and as Ann Herbert-Richardson points out, without steady work he often had a very thin time financially.

The Indian novelist Mulk Raj Anand, in an earlier Preface to *The Novel and the People* (Cobbett Press, 1944), writes of Fox's "sensitiveness," "intense preoccupation with ideas," and his "extremely modest presence, with his poet's pale face, his fine nose, delicate lips and gentle grey eyes." Both J. G. Crowther and Ann Herbert-Richardson also speak of Fox's gentleness. Crowther comments:

For me he was a gentle friend, and like his father, a man of ability and decision.

His gentleness made some difficulties for him in personal relationships, causing him to be uncertain of how to act because of the pain it might cause. In impersonal affairs he acted with clarity and courage, his participation in the Spanish Civil War and his death being consonant with his character.

Again, it would probably be unwise to set these two aspects of his character in opposition to each other: it seems more likely that Fox's humane gentleness and deep-rooted humanism led him to a belief in the need for courageous and firm action to oppose those who trampled on the values he held most dear.

Ann Herbert-Richardson had met Fox in 1934 when he came to write a story for the *Daily Worker* on the Unigar strike which she was then leading.

For seven weeks of the strike he came to Tottenham each day, giving encouragement and guidance to 300 girls and women, whose solidarity in their first struggle for better wages and conditions won his admiration.

The strike over, Fox became a tutor for many of the strikers, leading a series of discussion meetings on "The Class Struggle," held in Ann Herbert-Richardson's tiny room in North London. She remembers:

When I first attended one of his lectures I was much taken with the way he talked to the students. We were all factory workers, just becoming interested in the trade union movement and learning for the first time of the link between industrial action and political thought. It wasn't easy for Ralph, with his academic education and environment to explain his thoughts to us. But he tried very hard. His sympathetic approach, his gentleness of character made young people feel at ease with him, and he kept his little class together—where others had failed.

Fox's political activities did not cut him off from cultural and leisure pastimes; it is clear that he read an enormous amount, and Ann Herbert-Richardson recalls:

Ralph loved music and country walking. When he could afford it we would go to the Proms, especially to evenings of Beethoven and Brahms—that is, if there were no meetings to prevent us.

A. L. Morton worked for about a year with Fox on the *Daily Worker*, and speaks of him as a "lively, pleasant person to talk to with a very wide spread of interests."

T. A. Jackson also wrote interestingly of his work with Fox and their discussions about literature in an essay in the memorial volume *Ralph Fox: A Writer in Arms*.* Fox's journalistic writings show considerable versatility, ranging from thoughtful book reviews to more polemical, hard-hitting contributions to the "Worker's Diary" column in the *Daily Worker*, which he took over for a short period while its regular writer, Walter Holmes, was in Abyssinia covering the Italian invasion.

Fox went to Spain to fight with the International Brigade in late 1936, travelling first to Paris and then on to Spain through France in two special coaches. A letter of his printed in the memorial volume speaks of people saluting these coaches with clenched fists throughout their journey. Once in Spain he quickly assumed the responsibilities of a Political Commissar. Number 1 Company of the British Battalion was being formed and trained in Madrigueras near Albacete in December 1936. Some of Fox's letters printed in the memorial volume date from this time. Tom Wintringham, in his book on the Spanish Civil War, *English Captain* (1939), speaks of Fox explaining to his company that theirs was an army like none that had existed before, in which a dozen nationalities had to some extent to learn to give up their own peculiar habits and to tolerate the peculiar habits of others. He also warned them against drunkenness, asking if they had seen a drunken Spaniard since being in Spain. Alongside such memories of Fox's qualities of political leadership, he is remembered variously as the man who could organize anything from a political meeting to a soup kitchen, and as the possessor of a valuable sense of humour.

Fox went into action on Christmas Day 1936, advancing with the XIV International Brigade, which was mainly French, but included a British Company. They advanced

* Edited by John Lehmann, C. Day Lewis and T. A. Jackson, Lawrence and Wishart, 1937.

towards Lopera, near Andújar, but were forced to retreat because of heavy artillery and air attacks. Fox was killed going forward to inspect their position. As a tribute to his heroism the Battalion was given the name "Ralph Fox." As Bill Alexander, later Commander of the British Battalion, put it, there is no doubt that Fox displayed qualities of exemplary courage and leadership.

The Novel and the People, published posthumously, is of course in part a product of "thirties Marxism," but it is also a work to which Fox's whole life and experience contributed. Fox had written a fascinating essay entitled "Literature and Life" from a Marxist perspective for the journal *Plebs* as early as 1922; the essay is preceded by a short syllabus on "Historical Materialism and Literature" which, although not specifically ascribed to Fox, bears all the marks of his composition. The names in the syllabus and the essay include many that reappear fifteen years later in *The Novel and the People*, and the closing lines of the essay show how much of the foundation of this later work had been laid in the previous decade:

The student, moreover, will find in literature an exact mirror of contemporary life through all ages, and from the study of this raw material of social history can draw his own inevitable conclusions. But in this respect one last word. Let the working-class student beware of fixing class names to art. In dealing with great artists such words as feudal, bourgeois, proletarian, *may* lose all real significance. Let us remember that the greatest work is all inspired by pity for the common sufferings of humanity, and that a worker may obtain as much—probably more—enjoyment from a play by "feudal" Shakespeare as from the work of any so-called "proletarian" artist.

For while a great poet may be essentially the child of his age he yet rises above that age to become the possession of humanity in so far as he relates his age to the eternal stream of life ("Literature and Life" in *Plebs*, June 1922, p. 174).

The integration of the different elements in this con-
clusion is by no means perfect, and doubtless Fox in 1936
might have disagreed with some of the terminology he
used in the earlier piece; nevertheless much that is
positive in *The Novel and the People* can be traced back to
positions stated in the *Plebs* essay.

Fox was certainly a lover of the novel of long standing;
in *People of the Steppes* he recalls reading *Moby Dick* while
in the Soviet Union, and approaching its end with "relief
and dismay", which leads him to list the books he would
have liked to have had with him:

They were very few—Rabelais that magnificent purge, *Tristram
Shandy* and *Tom Jones*, Charles de Coster's *Tyl Eulenspiegel*,
and, strangely enough, *Jude the Obscure* (p. 63).

Moreover, Fox's interest in fiction was both appreciative
and critical; some of his early reviews in the *Sunday* and
Daily Worker are evidence of an early interest in the
development of a Marxist theory of the novel. In a review
of Dreiser's *The Titan* in the *Sunday Worker* of 12 August
1928, he makes a comment which perhaps indicates why,
of all literary forms, it is the novel which catches his
imagination:

"The social institutions under which the people of a certain
historical period and of a certain country are living are
dependent on these two forms of production; partly on the
development of labour, partly on that of the family," Engels
writes. The great novelist is the one who closely observes these
two forces at work in his own country and historical period,
and their reactions on individuals. Labour, and the family,
that is broadly the development of sex, are the themes which
only the novel, of all art forms, can deal with adequately.
Dreiser is, unconsciously, a Marxian novelist.

The final refusal to equate a writer's conscious outlook
and intention with the achievement of his work—for
which Fox found a justification in the writings of Marx

and Engels—is repeated in Fox's obituary for Rudyard Kipling published in the *Daily Worker* of 20 January 1936:

> Engels, writing of Balzac, long ago warned us against judging a great writer purely by his political and philosophical outlook. Some of the greatest have been the most childish and crude in their ideas.
>
> All the reactionary elements of imperialism are present in exaggerated form in Kipling's work.

Fox nevertheless finds much to praise in this work.

Fox also warned against attempting to relate art and literature to an economic base in a crude and mechanistic way in his essay "The Relation of Literature to Dialectical Materialism," published in the 1934 collection *Aspects of Dialectical Materialism*. His own creative work certainly followed his own critical advice. His early play for children, *Captain Youth* (1922), restricts its didactic element to a humorous libertarian appeal for children to be allowed to kiss and "make love" (a phrase which had not, at that time, such a clinical meaning as today) with one another after dark. His first—and, I think, better—novel, *Storming Heaven*, is again noteworthy for its undidactic celebration of human richness and diversity. Much of its action takes place in the young Soviet Union, and the characters come over as real people, not as pegs to hang political lessons upon. The hero ends up being imprisoned for murder, in spite of which Fox manages to retain the reader's sympathy for him.

The period of the Popular Front, with its clear message that the fight against fascism was a fight for all humanity and not just for the Communists or the working class, seems to have inspired Fox in many different ways, and to have encouraged him to return to his old love—the novel—with new insight and enthusiasm.

It is striking that Fox seems to draw his inspiration in *The Novel and the People* more from contemporary political events than from contemporary Marxist criticism. Admittedly the major work of Christopher Caudwell, Alick West and Georg Lukács was not available to Fox when he wrote the book, but *Problems of Soviet Literature*,* containing speeches by Gorki, Radek, Bukharin, Zhdanov and others, had been published in Britain in 1935 and, as far as the novel was concerned, R. D. Charques's *Contemporary Literature and Social Revolution* (1933) had contained a pioneering chapter on "The Bourgeois Novel." *Left Review* and *International Literature* had also printed many articles on Marxist attitudes and approaches to literature by 1937.

Fox refers directly to none of these in *The Novel and the People*; instead he reacts against spokesmen of the cultural élite such as David Garnett, and draws his inspiration from the politics of the age: Dimitrov in Leipzig, the Popular Front in France. In Dimitrov, in particular, many must have found an inspiring symbol not only of incredibly brave, but of *successful* resistance to fascism. An additional factor that probably endeared Dimitrov to Fox was the Bulgarian Communist's attack on jargon and mere phrase-making. In Dimitrov's speech on "Unity of the Working Class against Fascism" to the Seventh World Congress of the Comintern in 1935, he touched on matters close to Fox's heart:

We must mercilessly root out the weakness, not infrequently observed among our comrades, for cut-and-dried schemes, lifeless formulas and ready-made patterns. We must put an end to the state of affairs in which Communists, when lacking the knowledge or ability for Marxist-Leninist analysis, substitute for it general phrases and slogans such as "the revolutionary way out of the crisis . . ." (Reprinted in Georgi Dimitrov, *Selected Works*, vol. 1, Sofia, 1967, p. 641.)

* Reissued as *Soviet Writers' Congress, 1934*, Lawrence and Wishart, 1977.

Fox's own short essay "Think before Writing," published in *Communist Review* in March 1929 and reprinted in the memorial volume, is evidence of a comparable commitment to the need to communicate clearly and comprehensibly, and to avoid what T. A. Jackson, writing in that volume, describes as the "two besetting sins of British Marxist writers—the substitution of a Party jargon for living English; and its concomitant: the substitution of fossilized and frozen concepts for real thinking."

In *The Novel and the People* Fox quotes Lenin's dictum that truth "is formed out of the *totality of all* aspects of a phenomenon of reality, and their (mutual) *relationship*." He also insists on the fact that truth is reached through, not by avoiding, practical activity. These interrelated elements: activity, totality, relationship, are central to *The Novel and the People*. For Fox the novel is a powerful weapon in the battle for a knowledge of reality, first because it is the product and record of its creator's "intense investigation of an object," and second because —of all art forms—it can most fully *depict* reality in its totality and its interrelationships.

Fox has interesting things to say of the then still immature art form of the cinema, to which he is sympathetic but in which he fails to find the full potentiality for the depiction of the wholeness and totality of life and reality he discovers in the novel:

the novel will always have the advantage of being able to give a completer picture of man, of being able to show that important inner life, as distinct from the purely dramatic man, the acting man, which is beyond the scope of the cinema (p. 43).

Fox sees the novel as the worthy successor to the epic because it is the supreme art form of its age, able more fully to unite the abstract and the concrete, the subjective and objective, than any other form. The epic did not concern itself with the isolated individual or with private life, but this was because the society which produced it did not contain isolated individuals or "private lives" in the way capitalist society did:

The novel deals with the individual, it is the epic of the struggle of the individual against society, against nature, and it could only develop in a society where the balance between man and society was lost, where man was at war with his fellows or with nature (p. 44).*

The paradox that Fox explores at some length is that capitalist society creates the novel form, with its enormous potential for examining inner and outer realities and their relationships, but then prevents the novel from realizing this potential (see particularly the passage on Fielding, Richardson and Sterne on page 60).

We could perhaps add that Fielding's concentration on men and a "masculine" world of action, and Richardson's on women and on a "feminine" world of sentiment and passive analysis, mirror the divisions of the society which produced both writers and of which they write. Fox mentions sex-antagonism as one of a number of factors arising from the contradictions of capitalist society which prevent the growth of a world literature, and the same can perhaps be said of the age of Fielding and Richardson.

Fox is critical of all failure to depict totality and relationship in the novel: he criticizes Sholokhov's Communist heroes, who have

energy, force, will-power, they are alive and they are convincing, but they are nevertheless flat surfaces, rather than men in the round (p. 112).

But if the new Soviet and Socialist novels often fail to

* Those interested in Fox's comparisons between epic and novel will find a useful discussion of similar issues by Arnold Kettle in his Open University Course Unit, *The Late Nineteenth-Century Novel* (Open University Press, Course A 302 unit 23, Milton Keynes, 1973).

achieve an inner depiction of their characters, "modernist" writing is criticized by Fox for what he sees as the more serious failure—that of abstracting a part of life and experience from its social and historical context, seen in its tendency to approach the problem of creation

by means of the isolation of life from reality, and eventually, through the destruction of time and the inner logic of events, [as a result of which] the mutual interaction of the characters and the outer world is lost; it is an approach which in the end kills creation by denying the historical character of man (pp. 90–1).

This is strikingly reminiscent of Lukács, and it is worth turning briefly to Lukács's 1938 essay "Realism in the Balance," which starts, significantly, with a quotation from Dimitrov concerning the need for a new Cervantes, and praises Thomas Mann because:

he knows how thoughts and feelings grow out of the life of society and how experiences and emotions are parts of the total complex of reality. As a realist he assigns these parts to their rightful place within the total life context. He shows what area of society they arise from and where they are going to (Ernst Bloch and others, *Aesthetics and Politics*, New Left Books, 1977, p. 36).

Fox's comments on the artistic *type* (p. 34)—like Lukács's doubtless inspired by Engels's letters to Minna Kautsky and Margaret Harkness—also closely resemble some of Lukács's formulations. We are, I think, dealing here not with direct influences, but with a common reaction to contemporary events, a common development of shared basic positions. Here again, in Fox's comments on Falstaff, Don Quixote, Tom Jones, Julien Sorel and Proust's Monsieur de Charlus, we see the stress on totality and relationship.

Fox is by no means unaware of what present-day Marxists would call the "problem of ideology." He recognizes that the novel is the product of capitalist society, and that capitalist society controls—or attempts to control—the ideas that circulate within it. But Fox makes the important distinction between the forces of production, which were developed initially by the bourgeoisie, and the relations of production, to conceal which the free flow of ideas is restricted by the bourgeoisie. For Fox, the novel is as much the product of the genuine knowledge of the world gained through the "praxis" of developing the productive forces, as it is the record of blindnesses and misperceptions resulting from the need to conceal the exploitation of man by man. His comments on the changing balance of truth and falsity in the novel of the eighteenth and nineteenth centuries are interesting, as is his conclusion:

the Victorian writer could not discuss the real relations between men and women without tearing the veil off the real relations between man and man in society (p. 67).

With this present reissue of *The Novel and the People* the contemporary reader has easy access, for the first time in forty or so years, to the most important works of Ralph Fox, Christopher Caudwell and Alick West—the most significant English Marxist writers on literature of the 1930s. This means that students of the period can now see for themselves that the claim that English Marxist literary criticism of the period was purely sectarian, mechanical and Stalinist is wide of the mark. Perhaps, too, we can find something in the works of those critics that is largely absent from that of our contemporaries. That quality is surely the *comprehensiveness* of their work, the sheer scale of the questions and issues they confronted. Is not much of the literary criticism (sometimes even the Marxist literary criticism) of our own time guilty of isolating aspects of life from their dynamic interconnectedness and indissolubility? Fox's book, like his life, is a moving reminder to us that the overcoming of divisions, the achievement of unity, is a task for the active, not the passively contemplative.

My thanks are due to a number of individuals and organizations without whom this preface could not have been written. Ann Herbert-Richardson, A. L. Morton, Margot Heinemann, J. G. Crowther and Jack Lindsay contributed details of Fox's life and works; Bill Alexander, Joe Monks, Bobby Qualie and Sam Russell answered questions about the Spanish Civil War and the International Brigade, and the resources of the *Morning Star* library and the British Library were useful in tracking down some of Fox's more hard-to-obtain work. I have also made full use of the information contained in the preface to the German translation of *The Novel and the People* by Georg Seehase (*Der Roman und das Volk*, Dietz Verlag, East Berlin, 1975), from which I have taken many of the significant dates in Fox's life. Unless otherwise stated all comments made by and attributed to individuals have been made in personal communications to me.

JEREMY HAWTHORN

THE NOVEL AND THE PEOPLE

CHAPTER I

INTRODUCTION

THIS essay makes no pretension to deal with the whole vast field of the relation between art and life. It has a more limited aim, to examine the present position of the English novel, to try to understand the crisis of ideas which has destroyed the foundation on which the novel seemed once to rest so securely, and to see what is its future.

At this point I might perhaps say that I do believe that the novel has a future, even though it has only a very shaky present. It is the great folk art of our civilization, the successor to the epic and the *chanson de geste* of our ancestors, and it will continue to live. Life, however, means change; possibly, in art at least, not always a change for the better, but change nevertheless. It is the changes which must take place in the novel if it is to retain its vitality that are to be the subject of this book.

New arts have been born in the course of the history of man, like the cinema, for instance, but so far no art has ever completely died out. Man clings to every extension of his consciousness, to everything which enables him to heighten his sensitivity to the real world in which he lives. The novel is also a new art. True, its roots go back very far, to Trimalchio's Banquet, to Daphnis and Chloe, perhaps even further, to Herodotus. But the novel as an art in its own right, with its own rules, with its universal acceptance and appreciation, is a creature of our own civilization, a creature, above all, of the printing press.

It is only a part of literature, that is true, but so in a

sense, is the drama, and none would deny the drama its dignity as an art in its own right. The novel is not merely fictional prose, it is the prose of man's life, the first art to attempt to take the whole man and give him expression. Mr. E. M. Forster has pointed out that the great feature which distinguishes the novel from the other arts is that it has the power to make the secret life visible. It gives, therefore, a different view of reality from that given by poetry, or the drama, or the cinema, or painting, or music.

All these can express aspects of reality beyond the reach of the novel. But none of them can quite so satisfactorily express the full life of the individual man, woman or child. The why and wherefore of this I shall deal with elsewhere in this essay. Here I must be contented to state the fact and ask the reader to accept it for the moment.

Is there really such a crisis in the art of the novel that people must write books about it, cry shrilly to attract attention as you do when you see someone taking a direction you know must lead them into danger? Yes, most people professionally concerned are by now agreed that the English novel is in a sad state, that it has, in fact, lost direction and purpose. The novel, which above all depends on the fact that it is widely read, is rapidly becoming unreadable.

Of course, this does not imply a stay-in strike on the shelves of the tuppenny libraries. More novels are read to-day than ever before, but it is the unreadable which is read. Since paradox is not a meal for a hungry man, I will try to explain the position as I see it.

First, there is a crisis of quality. Certainly there were never so many writers producing excellent popular novels, those that tickle our immediate fancy, that we read with pleasure when the wireless is turned off (or even when it is turned on), or in the train, or at the seaside, read them once and never again, unless by sheer accident, having quite forgotten, till half-way through, that we had read them before. These novels, except very incidentally, do not, however, concern us here, for they do not deal with reality.

Naturally, their authors try to picture a real world, but the amount of reality achieved, unless by some accident of individual circumstance having nothing to do with the author, something in the reader and not in the book, is not sufficient to produce that violent shock which brings us, all our emotions taut, our mind alert, into the country of those who see, and having seen through their eyes, we never forget the experience.

To-day the novel-reviewer ploughs week after weary week through dismal acres of printed pages only to shrink from the second-rate emotions and adolescent relationships in cynical disgust. Mr. Cyril Connolly, franker than most reviewers, tells us he often finds it all but impossible to read the books he reviews, while his amusing articles are generally, fortunately for us, much more concerned with Mr. Connolly than with that melancholy raw material which provides Mr. Connolly with his inadequate daily bread.

Strangely enough, the spate of bad books is not due to the increase in the reading public. It is made possible by the way in which the tastes of that ever-growing public are being served by the publishers. The reader no longer gets what he likes, he has to like what he gets from the publishing colossus.

These immense and highly rationalized concerns, often possessing their own printing and binding works, and usually also that essential condition of modern business, a healthy overdraft on the bank, are compelled to seek books to keep them going. They must have more and more books, preferably novels, for the author of a novel need not be paid as much as the author of non-fiction, his book can be more cheaply produced and is sure of a ready market in the libraries if it can be guaranteed free of all originality.

The publishers must have more and more titles on their lists as part of their competitive war with one another, they must print more books in order to keep their print shops busy, or, where they do not own their own print shops, to satisfy the printer who undertakes their business. What they print is not of great concern. It will be printed in the same type, on the same paper, bound in the same cloth, given the same dust jacket and sold to the same libraries, whether it be rubbish or a hidden masterpiece. In either case the publisher in his "blurb" will acclaim it a masterpiece, and most reviewers, having long ago abandoned the hopeless task of discrimination, will wearily accept the publisher's valuation at a greater or less discount, according to the mood of the moment or their personal relation to the publisher concerned.

The author himself has become a mere cipher in this great game of making publishing pay. When his books sell he is made into an important person, which gives him some independence, but he is still only a part of the game, transferred to the publicity side of the business. The commercial side will now treat him with some deference, but deference, properly handled, can also be made to pay.

Much could be said about the publicity aspect, about the various book of the month clubs, about back-scratching, about the art of managing the Press, about the "services" of broadcasting to literature, but there would be little point in it, so far as the objects of this essay are concerned.

What we are interested in, as author and reader, is the fact that publishing is now an integral part of big business. It would be foolish to blame the publishers, who have been forced into the position by what our parents used to call "the facts of life." It is only necessary to note that the effect on literature, and particularly on the novel, has been deplorable. Quality has vanished from the aims of the book business and quantity has taken its place.

There is, however, an even more important crisis, a crisis of outlook among the novelists themselves. Despite the terrible flood of bad novels and poor work, there are good novelists, honest workmen, producing to-day. It is only a very short time since D. H. Lawrence died. James Joyce and E. M. Forster are still alive. Rebecca West, Aldous Huxley and half a dozen others are still seriously and conscientiously writing novels, with what degree of success we are not here concerned.

The difficulties facing the serious writer to-day are profound ones. A writer more than any other artist expresses his country. His novels are translated and read throughout the world. The England of yesterday was judged abroad by Wells, Kipling, Galsworthy and Conrad. The England of to-day is judged by Huxley chiefly, and after him by a few younger writers whose works are just winning recognition in translation.

The novelist, therefore, has a special responsibility both to the present and the past of his country. What he inherits from the past is important, because it shows what are the sections of his country's cultural heritage which have meaning to-day. What he says of the present is important, because he is assumed to be expressing what is most vital in the spirit of his time. It may be objected that the novelist is not concerned with other people's attitude to his work. What he inherits, what he expresses, is strictly his own affair.

Even if it is his affair alone, he cannot, however, cut himself off from the outside world's reactions to his work. In a world where nationalism has run mad in its most egoistic and destructive forms, the attitude of a serious and important writer towards nationalism is an important one. To their infinite credit it can be said that every serious English writer of to-day understands this and that the majority of them are very seriously concerned about the problems involved.

Shall the writer renounce his country for a religion? Mr. Evelyn Waugh has done this, only to find that it lands him in the receptive lap of another country's nationalism. Apparently to-day Roman Catholicism implies support for Fascist Italy, the most aggressive and egoistically brutal, after Germany, of all modern States. Shall he accept the logical consequences of D. H. Lawrence's blood and race cult? Then he may end by supporting Nazi culture with its arguments of the mediaeval torture chamber and its "spiritual" glorification of war.

Mr. Waugh has written the life of Edmund Campion, the Jesuit martyr, and been crowned with the Hawthornden prize, one of the two distinctions it is possible for an English author to win. But would Shakespeare or Marlowe have considered Campion a martyr? Or would they not have inclined to the view that his activities, at a time when England was fighting for national existence, fighting for the conditions which created our national culture, were best characterized by Shakespeare's reference to:

the fools of time,
Which die for goodness, who have liv'd for crime.

Clearly, the writer of to-day has to distinguish very sharply between what is truly national and what is merely nationalistic or anti-national. The past matters as much as the present. We must carry it with us on our march and therefore we are concerned that the burden should not weigh us down too heavily, that we should be able to choose from the past what is real enough to be of help, and abandon, for the time, what can only be a hindrance.

The crisis of outlook is concerned with philosophy, and

therefore with form. Since the War the philosophical outlook of most English writers has been deeply influenced by that last of European liberals, Sigmund Freud.* Psycho-analysis, as developed by Freud, is the apotheosis of the individual, the extreme of intellectual anarchy. It has certainly affected the English novel in the last twenty years more than any other body of ideas. It has also brought it to a state of almost complete intellectual bankruptcy, even though some strikingly original work also owes much of its force to the revelation of the individual made possible by Freudian analysis.

The last point which troubles the mind of the writer to-day is what I will call the social question. Can a novelist remain indifferent to the problems of the world in which he lives? Can he shut his ears to the clamour of preparing war, his eyes to the state of his country, can he keep his mouth closed when he sees horror around him and life being denied daily in the name of a State pledged to maintain the sanctity of private greed?

More and more novelists are beginning to feel that eyes, ears and voice are, in fact, organs of sense, responsive to the stimulus of the human world, and not mere passive servants of a spiritual world supposed traditionally to be the domain of "art." They understand that they live in a time in which nothing less than the fate of humanity is being decided, and they deeply resent the suggestion that man's fate is not the concern of those whose traditional pride has always been their humanism.

They are aware that there are two important views as to the future of civilization. One view believes that civilization will continue to develop on the basis of private property, war and insane egoism expressed in the dictatorial nationalist state. The other view believes that humanity is fighting for a new series of values based on social property, which shall banish war, destroy national-

* The phrase is borrowed from Mr. Day Lewis.

ism, and replace it by the free growth of healthy nations co-operating with one another in a world civilization.

Most writers, to a greater or less degree, incline to the second view. Some of them, more clear-sighted than others, feel that such a new civilization will come largely as a result of the struggle now being led by the working-class and that the beginnings of that new civilization are already apparent in the Soviet Union. This has made them interested in Marxism, the outlook on life of the revolutionary section of the working-class and of the great Union of Socialist Republics with its 170 million inhabitants.

The view has hitherto prevailed that though the working-class movement and the Russian Revolution might be good in themselves, Marxism, because it is a "materialist" philosophy, is a philosophy hostile to artistic expression. This view is generally put in the form of suggesting that Marxism "binds the artist in chains of dogma."

Perhaps that is no longer stated with quite the same conviction. People know more about Marxism to-day. But it prevails in general, and even among those who sympathize with Marxists there are many who still believe that such formulas as "socialist realism" or "revolutionary novel" are not to be accepted seriously save as political slogans.

It is the aim of this essay to show that the future of the English novel and therefore the solution to the problems which vex the English novelist lies precisely in Marxism with its artistic formula of a "socialist realism" which shall unite and re-vitalize the forces of the left in literature.

CHAPTER II

MARXISM AND LITERATURE

MARXISM is a materialist philosophy. It believes in the primacy of matter and that the world exists outside of us and independently of us. But Marxism also sees all matter as changing, as having a history, and accepts nothing as fixed and immutable. In the seventeenth century few English writers would have quarrelled with a materialist view of life, though their view of materialism would not have been the same as that of Marx and Engels. To Shakespeare, drawing his philosophical views from Rabelais and Montaigne, there would have appeared nothing outrageous in the Marxian view of life. For the greater part of the eighteenth century a materialist view of life would have been accepted without question by many of the greatest British writers.

It is not so to-day. It has not been so for more than a century. To-day the literary journalist protests that materialism and imagination cannot go to bed together. The result, they suggest, would not be creation, but simply an unholy row. It is a curiously perverted view, for it would appear to be the most natural thing in the world for the imaginative writer, and particularly the novelist, to adopt a materialist view of life.

"Being determines consciousness" is the Marxist definition of the ultimate relation between matter and spirit. Whether or not this is the actual view of the artist it must, in fact, be the basis of his creative work. For all imaginative creation is a reflection of the real world in which the creator lives. It is the result of his contact with that world and his love or hate for what he finds in that world.

It is the lights and colours, the forms and shapes, the breath of the winds, the scents of life, the physical beauty or the physical ugliness of animal life, including the lives of human beings, the acts, the thoughts, the dreams of actual men and women, including the creator himself, that form the stuff of art.

Milton demanded three things of poetry: that it be "simple, sensuous and passionate." Art that is not sensuous, that is not concerned with perception of the real world, with sensible objects, is not art at all—not even the shadow of art. The essence of the creative process is the struggle between the creator and external reality, the urgent demand to master and re-create that reality. "But does not Marxism claim that works of art are merely a reflection of economic needs and economic processes?" it will be objected.

No, this is not the view of Marxism, though it is the view of a number of materialists of the nineteenth century of the positivist school whose views have nothing in common with Marxian, dialectical, materialism. Marx has clearly stated his ideas on the relationship between the spiritual processes of life, of which artistic creation is one, and the material basis of life, in the famous Preface to his *Critique of Political Economy*. Here is the passage:

"The mode of production of the material means of existence conditions the whole process of social, political and intellectual life. It is not the consciousness of men that determines their existence, but, on the contrary, their social existence that determines their consciousness. At a certain stage of their development, the material forces of production in society come in conflict with the existing relations of production, or—what is but a legal expression for the same thing—with the property relations within which they had been at work before. From forms of development of the forces of production these relations turn into their fetters. Then opens an epoch of social revolution. With the change of the economic foundation the entire immense superstructure is more or less rapidly transformed. In considering such revolutions the distinction should always be between the material revolution in the economic conditions of production which can be determined with the precision of natural science, and the juridical, political, religious, aesthetic, or philosophic—in short, ideological forms—in which men become conscious of this conflict and fight it out."

Marx, then, certainly believed that the material mode of life in the end determined the intellectual. But he never for a moment considered that the connection between the two was a direct one, easily observed and mechanically developing. He would have laughed to scorn the idea that because capitalism replaces feudalism, therefore a "capitalist" art immediately replaces "feudal" art, and that all great artists must in consequence directly reflect the needs of the new capitalist class. Nor, as will appear later, did he consider that because the capitalist mode of production was a more progressive one than the feudal, capitalist art must therefore always stand on a higher level than feudal art, while feudal art in turn must stand above the art of the slave States of Greece and Rome, or the ancient Eastern monarchies. Such crude and vulgar views are foreign to the whole spirit of Marxism.

Changes in the material basis of society, Marx rightly urged, can be determined by the economic historian with the precision of natural science (which, of course, is not the same thing as saying that these changes are scientifically determined). But no such scientific measurement of the resulting changes in the social and spiritual superstructure of life is possible. The changes take place, men become conscious of them, they "fight out" the conflict between old and new in their minds, but they do so unevenly, burdened by all kinds of past heritage, often unclearly, and always in such a way that it is not easy to trace the changes in men's minds.

It is true, for example, that the *Code Napoléon* is the legal expression of the social and economic changes wrought by the French Revolution. Yet the knowledge of this does not in itself explain the *Code Napoléon*. One must understand also the past history of France and the relation of classes in that country before the Revolution, one must understand the course of the Revolution itself and the changes in class relationships which the Revolution brought about, and finally, one must understand Napoleon's military dictatorship. Then only does the *Code* become comprehensible as the legal expression of the new bourgeois society and the French industrial revolution which began during the Napoleonic period. And law is perhaps the most responsive part of the ideal superstructure, it changes most easily in accordance with changes in the mode of production. But art is much farther from the basis, responds far less easily to the changes in it.

Engels in a letter to J. Bloch written in 1890, was quite emphatic about this point. "According to the materialist conception of history," he wrote, "the determining element in history is *ultimately* the production and reproduction in real life. More than this neither Marx nor I have ever asserted. If therefore somebody twists this into the statement that the economic element is the *only* determining one, he transforms it into a meaningless, abstract and absurd phrase. The economic situation is the basis, but the various elements of the superstructure—political forms of the class struggle and its consequences, constitutions established by the victorious class after a successful battle, etc.—forms of law—and then even the reflexes of all these actual struggles in the brains of the combatants: political, legal, philosophical theories, religious ideas and their further development into systems of dogma—also exercise their influence upon the course of the historical struggles and in many cases preponderate in determining their *form*. There is an interaction of all these elements, in which, amid all the endless *host* of accidents (i.e., of things and events whose inner connection is so remote or so impossible to prove that we regard it as absent and can neglect it), the economic movement finally asserts itself as necessary. Otherwise the application of the theory to any period of history one chose would be easier than the solution of a simple equation of the first degree."

Marxism, therefore, while reserving the final and decisive factor in any change for economic causes, does not deny that "ideal" factors can also influence the course of history and may even preponderate in determining the *form* which changes will take (but only the form). It is only a caricature of Marxism to suggest that it under-estimates the importance of such a spiritual factor in human consciousness as artistic creation, or to make the absurd claim that Marx considered works of art to be the direct reflection of material and economic causes. He did not. He understood perfectly well that religion, or philo-sophy, or tradition can play a great part in the creation of a work of art, even that any one of these or other "ideal" factors may preponderate in determining the *form* of the work in question. Among all the elements which go to make a work of art it is, however, only the economic movement which asserts itself as *finally* necessary, for what Marx and Engels considered to be true of historical changes they also considered true of aesthetic creation.

It is often objected against Marxism that it denies the individual, who is merely the prey of abstract economic forces which drive him to his doom with the inevitability of a Greek fate. We will leave aside the question of whether or not the conception that man is driven by external fate to an inevitable end makes the creation of a work of art impossible. Perhaps Calvinism has never produced great art, but the idea of doom and fate has done so—in the Greek tragedies, in the works of Hardy, to mention only two instances. It is nevertheless possible that the objection, if it really represented the Marxian view, would be a valid one. At least this objection is prompted by the humanist tradition of the great art of the western world, and is therefore worthy of respect, even though it is based on a grave misunderstanding.

For Marxism does not deny the individual. It does not see only masses in the grip of inexorable economic forces. True, some Marxist literary works, particularly some "proletarian" novels, have given innocent critics cause to believe that this is the case, but here perhaps the weakness has been in the novelists who have failed to rise to the greatness of their theme of man changing himself through the process of changing nature and creating new economic forces. Marxism places man in the centre of its philosophy, for while it claims that material forces may change man, it declares most emphatically that it is man who changes the material forces and that in the course of so doing he changes himself.

Man and his development is the centre of the Marxist philosophy. How does man change? What are his relations with the external world? These are the questions to which the founders of Marxism have sought and found answers. I do not wish here to outline Marxist philosophy, for that is done more capably elsewhere; but let us examine for a moment this question of man as an active historical agent, man at work and struggling with life, for this is the man who is at once artistic creator and the object of art. This is the way in which Engels explained the part of the individual in history:

"History makes itself in such a way that the final result always arises from conflicts between many individual wills, of which each again has been made what it is by a host of particular conditions of life. Thus there are innumerable intersecting forces, an infinite series of parallelograms of forces which give rise to one resultant—the historical event. This again may itself be viewed as the product of a power which, taken as a whole, works *unconsciously* and without volition. For what each individual wills is obstructed by everyone else, and what emerges is something that no one willed. Thus past history proceeds in the manner of a natural process and is also essentially subject to the same laws of movement. But from the fact that individual wills—of which each desires what he is impelled to by his physical constitution and external, in the last resort economic, circumstances (either his own personal circumstances or those of society in general)—do not attain what they want, but are merged into a collective mean, a common resultant, it must not be concluded that their value $= O$. On the contrary, each contributes to the resultant and is to this degree involved in it."

Here is not only a formula for the historian, but also for the novelist. For the one concern of the novelist is, or should be, this question of the individual will in its conflict with other wills on the battleground of life. It is the fate of man that his desires are never fulfilled, but it is also his glory, for in the effort to obtain their fulfilment he changes, be it ever so little, in ever so limited a degree, life itself. Not $X = O$ is the Marxist formula for the fate of man, but "on the contrary, each contributes to the resultant and is to this degree involved in it."

The conflict of wills, of desires and passions, is not, however, a conflict of abstract human beings, for Engels is careful to emphasize that man's desires and actions are conditioned by his physical constitution and, finally, by economic circumstances, either his personal circumstances or those of society in general. In his social history it is, in the last resort again, the class to which he belongs, the psychology of that class, with its contradictions and conflicts, which plays the determining part. So that each man has, as it were, a dual history, since he is at the same time a type, a man with a social history, and an individual, a man with a personal history. The two, of course, even though they may be in glaring conflict, are also one, a unity, in so far as the latter is eventually conditioned by the former, though this does not and should not imply that in art the social type must dominate the individual personality. Falstaff, Don Quixote, Tom Jones, Julien Sorel, Monsieur de Charlus, are all types, but they are types in whom the social characteristics constantly reveal the individual, and in whom the personal hopes, hungers, loves, jealousies and ambitions in turn light up the social background.

The novelist cannot write his story of the individual fate unless he also has this steady vision of the whole. He must understand how his final result arises from the individual conflicts of his characters, he must in turn understand what are the manifold conditions of life which have made each of those individuals what she or he is. "What emerges is something that no one willed." How exactly that sums up each great work of art, and how well it expresses the pattern of life itself, since behind the event that no one willed a pattern does exist. Marxism gives to the creative artist the key to reality when it shows him how to discern that pattern and the place which each individual occupies in it. At the same time it consciously gives to man his full value, and in this sense is the most humanist of all world outlooks.

CHAPTER III

TRUTH AND REALITY

"I AM a man for whom the visible world exists," Théophile Gautier told the brothers Goncourt when he wished to explain the essence of himself as an artist. Had he said "I am a man for whom the world exists," he might not have explained so well his own virtues and limitations as a writer, but he would have given us a very good beginning for judging the relation between a writer and reality, for judging his attitude to truth. One example will show what I mean. André Gide, in the course of a literary confession, answers a critic who suggests that it was only during his journey in the French Congo, during 1925, that he became aware of social iniquity.

"This is not so," Gide replies. "If I had simply published the whole of my notes and the diary of my journey in the period when I wrote *Amyntas* (1893–96), in the same way as I did for my journey in the Congo, or, to be more exact, if I had given free play in my notes to everything that was on my mind at that time, you would have found in them, for example, the story of the commencement of the exploitation of the Gafsa phosphates, and, more than anything else, the story of the sinister and methodical expropriation of the small Arab farmers by the C— bank, none of which left me indifferent. But there you are! It was not *my job*. I should have thought myself dishonoured as an artist if I had lent my pen to such vulgar cares. That was something for people more competent in such affairs than myself."

In fact, André Gide was at that time a man for whom the world did not exist, except subjectively. It was not till much later, after the War, during his travels in the

Congo, that he began to perceive the world as it exists in reality, and not merely as it existed in his own consciousness. But even here, in the Congo, his approach was still subjective, still that of the outraged individual rather than of the man who sees steadily and whole. His own explanation is most interesting.

When he first saw colonial exploitation, in Algeria during the 'nineties, he had still, he says, "the absurd cult of the 'expert,' of the trained men, economists, administrators (or generals in war); I had confidence in them and gave them due credit. I thought that what aroused my indignation must make them indignant also and that they were better qualified than I to denounce and reform abuse, extortion, injustice and error. Then at that time I was still deplorably modest and did not yet understand that when there is no one but the victim to shout 'stop thief,' he runs the risk of not being heard. In the Congo it was different. Here I could have no illusion that there would be anyone to listen to the cry of the robbed. I had been told so over and over again before I left, in order to dissuade me from going. 'Don't go out there; nobody goes out there for pleasure.' Administrators, traders, missionaries, the only representatives of France, all had their mouths closed, either out of duty or self-interest. Here, where I alone was able to speak, I *had* to speak. I was no anti-imperialist when I left home, and it was not as an anti-imperialist that I denounced the abuses I had witnessed. Yes, it was not till much later that an unescapable logic led me to connect these particular abuses to a whole deplorable system and that I was brought to understand that a system which tolerated, protected and favoured such abuses because it profited from them itself, was bad from top to bottom."

In this confession Gide traces his whole progress from the subjective intellectual, unwilling to recognize any truth except through his own self-limited consciousness (his cult of the "expert"), to the gradual breaking down of his idealist standpoint as he comes to see, not merely that the outer world exists, which he had always known, but that it can be understood, and that it must be mastered before his individual consciousness finds its freedom. He had begun to understand that consciousness, which he had looked upon as the central fact of being, the activity which creates the world, was in fact merely the subjective side of human activity as a whole, that it was not something apart from objectivity, but was merely the refashioning of the objective world in his own mind and its translation into the language of thought.

It would seem as though the development of an ever-growing and ever more minute specialization and division of labour in the modern world had strangled the voice of the writer, blinded him to a complete vision of the real world. "My job is to write," is its narrowest expression, as though that job precluded all knowledge of other jobs. Poetry, Mr. Baldwin has assured us, is essentially a harmless vocation, so long, that is, as the poet shuts out from his vision all that part of life which might affect the "harmless" character of his work. This narrow view of the artist's function is a very modern one. Before the middle of the nineteenth century it would have been completely inacceptable to the majority of the world's writers. In the heroic period of English literature, from Marlowe to Fielding, it was unknown.

The revolutionary task of literature to-day is to restore its great tradition, to break the bonds of subjectivism and narrow specialization, to bring the creative writer face to face with his only important task, that of winning the knowledge of truth, of reality. Art is one of the means by which man grapples with and assimilates reality. On the forge of his own inner consciousness the writer takes the white-hot metal of reality and hammers it out, re-fashions it to his own purpose, beats it out madly by the violences of thought, to steal a phrase from Naomi Mitchison. The whole procession of creation, the whole agony of the artist, is in this violent conflict with reality in the effort to fashion a truthful picture of the world.

> Knowledge enormous makes a God of me.
> Names, deeds, grey legends, dire events, rebellions,
> Majesties, sovran voices, agonies,
> Creations and destroyings, all at once
> Pour into the wide hollows of my brain,
> And deify me, as if some blithe wine,
> Or bright elixir peerless I had drunk,
> And so become immortal.

Keats, hated and beset by the reactionary critics of his day with a vile ardour that was more furious even than that shown towards the more obviously revolutionary Byron and Shelley, has in his greatest poem, the poem he was unable to finish, attempted to give the very essence of the revolutionary struggle of the great creative artist. For the really great writer, regardless of his own political views, must always engage in a terrible and revolutionary battle with reality, revolutionary because he must seek to change reality. For him, his life is always a battle of heaven and hell, a conflict of gods dethroned and gods ascendant, a fight for the soul of man.

Can Marxism fit the writer for this battle? A recent leading article in *The Times Literary Supplement*, discussing American revolutionary literature, attempts an answer to the question. Can this new literature, asks *The Times* critic, "reach out to include and cope with the whole range of human experience? Clearly never so long as the dogmatists have their way. The aim of an ultimate art, and in its degree of all art whatsoever, is an understanding which comprehends all forms and creeds, and which cannot therefore of its nature bind itself to dwell within the limits of even a far more liberal social philo-

not this vital, youthful art create the epic of the new age?

It is impossible to deny that it may succeed in doing this to a great extent, but hardly, I think, altogether. For the novel will always have the advantage of being able to give a completer picture of man, of being able to show that important inner life, as distinct from the purely dramatic man, the acting man, which is beyond the scope of the cinema. Indeed, the challenge of the cinema may compel the novel to reassert itself by finding again important qualities which it has lost, above all by forcing it to face the need for action. It is not merely love of crime or violence which makes the detective novel popular. It corresponds to a real need for action in literature, for the dramatic, which the cinema has nourished and from which the modern novel shrinks.

The epic was a complete expression of a society in a way in which the novel never has been and never could be. There was a balance between the characters of the epic and the society in which they lived which has since been lost. Indeed, the *Iliad* is more a picture of a society than of any one of its characters, a society in which the individual does not feel himself in opposition to the collective, any more than he feels himself in conflict with nature. He is part of his society, and, at times, almost a part of nature, or else dominated by nature, but never in conflict with it or master of it. The *Chanson de Roland* also is a story of the conflict of two societies, in this case "Christians" and "Pagans" in which the characters, Charlemagne, Roland, Oliver, Ganelon, the traitor knight, are rather types than individuals, types of wisdom, courage, loyalty and treachery.

The story or tale, dealing with the woes and joys of individual men and women, with *private* life, comes only with the break-up of the old social life of Greco-Roman civilization, of the Celtic communities. The self-contained societies have gone and the tale is already a cosmopolitan thing, as in Daphnis and Chloe, or the story of Tristan and Iseult.

The novel deals with the individual, it is the epic of the struggle of the individual against society, against nature, and it could only develop in a society where the balance between man and society was lost, where man was at war with his fellows or with nature. Such a society is capitalist society. The two greatest stories in the world are the *Odyssey* and *Robinson Crusoe*. But how different they are! Odysseus lives in a society without history, a society in which myth and reality are indistinguishable and time is without terror. The sea-driven Odysseus knows that his fate is in the hands of the gods who control nature, for the storm is the wrath of Poseidon and shipwreck is only another trial in the long journey home to Ithaca.

Not so with Robinson Crusoe. "This eighteenth century individual," writes Marx, "constituting the joint product of the dissolution of the feudal form of society and of the new forces of production which had developed since the sixteenth century, appears as an ideal whose existence belongs to the past, not as a result of history, but as its starting point." Odysseus had no history. He lived in the childhood of the world and the gods were his familiars. Robinson renounced the past and prepared to make his own history, he was the new man who was ready to command nature, his enemy. Robinson's world is a real world, described with a vivid and understanding feeling for the value of material things. The storm is a horror which puts in peril the ship and its cargo, men are pirates and mutineers, cruel and merciless to their fellows, but Crusoe's faith in himself, his naïve optimism, enable him to overcome both his own folly in risking his fortune, the cruelty of nature and the savage hostility of his fellow men, and to found his ideal colony beyond the seas.

He tells the exiled Russian nobleman his story "of my living in the island; and how I managed both myself and the people that were under me, just as I have since minuted it down. They were exceedingly taken with the story, and especially the prince, who told me with a sigh, that the true greatness of life was to be masters of ourselves." So the long voyage of Crusoe, who mastered himself, came to an end, not in the return to Ithaca and the battle with the false suitors, not in the welcome of the patient Penelope and the wise Telemachus, but in that last journey to Siberia and the return to the Elbe.

"Here my partner and I found a very good sale for our goods, as well those of China as the sables, etc., of Siberia; and dividing the produce, my share amounted to three thousand four hundred and seventy-five pounds seventeen shillings and threepence, including about six hundred pounds' worth of diamonds which I purchased at Bengal." Robinson's life, like that of Odysseus, is the story of a strange journey, and like that of Odysseus it ends—"in retirement, and the blessing of ending our days in peace." But the whole aim of Odysseus is to return from the war at Troy to the island home, while with Robinson it is the outward, and not the homeward, trip in his voyage which is important. He is the empire-builder, the man who challenges nature and wins. His reward is calculated down to the last threepence, and it is well earned.

Throughout the eighteenth century *Robinson Crusoe* was used as the basis for lectures in political economy. Indeed, echoes of it are still heard in the work of John Stuart Mill. The new bourgeoisie had found its singer and he was not idle, nor was the lay he sang an empty one. He stood at the threshold of a new epoch in the life of man, when the world in the course of two centuries was to undergo its most complete transformation and man himself to fulfil the dreams of the ancient poets that he would fly in the air, span the earth in seven league boots, and master the seas above and below. In fulfilling these dreams man also transformed himself, destroying ancient and noble cultures, degrading the relations between man and man, putting the life of the mind on a lower lever than the trading of coal or boot polish, and covering the real character of man's life with a thick veil of hypocrisy such as had never before existed in relations between men.

Capitalist society as it has developed, has placed the artist in a totally different position from that which he occupied in all preceding social systems. In its early period, from the Renaissance to the middle of the eighteenth century, this was not so obvious. The writer was still free to see man as he is, to give a whole picture of him, and to criticize the present as well as the mediaeval past. In short, capitalism, which created realism as a method and gave it its perfect form in the novel, capitalism, which made man the centre of art, also in the end destroyed the conditions in which realism can flourish and only permitted man to appear in art, particularly in the novel, in a castrated or perverted form. Théophile Gautier summed up the position when, talking of the trial of Flaubert for indecency in 1857, he said: "Really, I blush for my trade! In return for the very modest sums which I have to earn, because I should otherwise die of hunger, I say only a half or a quarter of what I think . . . and yet at every sentence I run the risk of being dragged before the Courts." From *Jonathan Wild* to the trial of Flaubert and Gautier's bitter remark was only a few years more than a century, yet what had happened in that time!

The growth of capitalism, particularly the minute subdivision of labour and the increasing exploitation of man by man which followed on the establishment of machine industry and the expropriation of the independent producer, whether peasant or artisan, has resulted on the one hand in a general decay of art, which has been unable to produce anything to equal the great works of the Renaissance, that period of transition from feudalism to capitalism in which the individual won his right to life, or the equally great art of the slave society of Greece or Rome, or the Eastern feudalism of China; and on the other hand it has brought with it the degradation of the artist himself, crushed by the seemingly insoluble contradiction between the individual and society.

In the *Communist Manifesto* Marx and Engels have exposed the real causes of this decline in cultural life, describing the revolutionary part played by the bourgeoisie in destroying preceding social relations:

"The bourgeoisie, wherever it has got the upper hand, has put an end to all feudal, patriarchal, idyllic relations. It has pitilessly torn asunder the motley feudal ties that bound man to his 'natural superiors,' and has left no other bond between man and man than naked self-interest, than callous 'cash-payment.' It has drowned the most heavenly ecstasies of religious fervour, of chivalrous enthusiasm, of philistine sentimentalism, in the icy water of egotistical calculation. It has resolved personal worth into exchange value, and in place of the numberless indefeasible chartered freedoms, has set up that single, unconscionable freedom—Free Trade. In one word, for exploitation, veiled by religious and political illusions, it has substituted naked, shameless, direct, brutal exploitation.

"The bourgeoisie has stripped of its halo every occupation hitherto honoured and looked up to with reverent awe. It has converted the physician, the lawyer, the priest, the poet, the man of science, into its paid wage-labourers."

So, by depriving millions of small producers of their property, capitalism has achieved a tremendous levelling process. And the same levelling process has been brought into cultural relations. The individual whose labour power has become a commodity ceases to possess a moral or aesthetic value, and since commodity exchange equates all things, so art also becomes a commodity and is equated to its very opposite and antagonism. In the ancient or feudal societies, based upon slavery or serfdom as forms of exploitation, personal relations were more direct, dependence of one man upon another was immediate and personal also, the division of labour was a simple one and the individual was able to express himself directly in his handicraft work. In such societies art had a freshness and a vitality which has been largely lost.

Ruskin and William Morris understood this, but they made the great mistake of imagining that this freshness could be recaptured by a return to an artificial mediaevalism, instead of by a revolutionary destruction of the private property basis of capitalist society, a mistake from which Morris, under the influence of Marx, began to free himself in the last years of his life.

Creative artists in the nineteenth century felt very deeply the new, impersonal character of the relations between men arising from the concentration of capital. No less deeply did they feel the levelling of their work through the capitalist market. Money makes all things equal—a Michael Angelo to so much oil or soap, if it is purchased by a millionaire with a fortune made from these useful and homely commodities, a play by Shakespeare to a quantity of manure, should a season be run in the West End on the charity of a shareholder in the Imperial Chemical Industries. The nineteenth century novelist was inclined to resent these simple equations by a savage hatred of the new bourgeoisie. But his hatred blinded him to certain of the positive sides of the new society.

The modern millionaire and his image in the class of

which he is the pinnacle, is only made possible by the development of science, which he in turn assists because it is profitable to him. In this development of science and in the devoted lives of the discoverers of a new world, in Faraday, Pasteur and Curie, are the real poetry of our age, and the real heroes of our time. But the nineteenth century novelist, shocked by the bourgeois world in which he lived, disillusioned by the final shattering in 1848 of the great dreams of the French revolution, scared by the appearance of the working-class, is unable to see this. A typical attitude is that of the Goncourt brothers who write in their diary for 1857:

"No century has ever bluffed so much, even in the realm of science. For years now the Bilboquets of chemistry and physics have been promising us every morning a miracle, an element, a new metal, solemnly undertaking to warm us with copper plates in water, to feed us or kill us with something, to make us all centenarians, etc. All this is nothing but an immense bluff leading to the Institute, to decorations, to pensions, to the consideration of persons of consequence. And meanwhile, living goes up, doubles, trebles, increases tenfold, whilst the raw materials of nourishment are either lacking or else deteriorate, even death in war makes no progress (that was clear enough at Sebastopol) and a good bargain is always the worst bargain imaginable."

Well, scientists have since proved that they can make great progress in death and at present it is chiefly this negative aspect of their work which impresses the novelist. But science as a power to transform life, the great contradiction between the life and work of the scientist and the use made of them by capitalist society, these are still almost as much ignored by the novelist as materials for his art as they were by the Goncourt brothers.

Throughout the nineteenth century we find the artist engaging in a vain effort to deny the world which imposes

upon him standards he can never accept. Some do so by
building their ivory tower and hoisting from its summit
the silken banner of art for art's sake. This strange war-
cry is in fact a challenge to a civilization which denies
any value to art at all, save that of money. Art for art's
sake is the hopeless answer to art for money's sake, hope-
less since ivory was never a good material to choose for
fortification.

Some, like Gerard de Nerval, are driven to hang
themselves. Others, in desperation, deny their own work.
Rimbaud, youthful poet of the Paris Commune, hater of
the bourgeoisie and revolutionary experimenter in poetry,
buries himself alive in Abyssinia, with savage cynicism
trades in arms and human bodies, in all the products of
Africa at a time when these have become particularly
the objects of the greed of that bourgeoisie he loathed.
Gauguin retires to Tahiti to live with the primitive com-
munists of Polynesia and decorates his wattle hut with
masterpieces, while Cézanne flings his finished canvasses
into a ditch and Van Gogh ends up in an asylum for the
insane.

Yet at this very time their friend and defender, Émile
Zola, a vague but sincere genius, is darkly groping
towards the solution, feeling a new fire at work in him
as he comes nearer to the harsh and bitter, but passionate
life of the working-class. Zola fails, burdened as he is
with the false theories of his predecessors which he
develops into the fatal and mechanical doctrine of
naturalism. But it is a generous failure from which we
can learn much.

The secret was there, close at hand. Marx and Engels
had revealed how capitalism, in destroying the conditions
in which great art can flourish, also creates the conditions
in which it becomes possible for art to attain greater
heights than ever before in man's history. Yet capitalism
is itself incapable of making use of those conditions, of

giving birth to this new art. It has for the first time in history created the conditions for a world art, a world literature. It has subdued the whole world to its image, it has so developed technique and production that there is no more reason for the existence of "backward" and "advanced" peoples. I will quote the *Communist Manifesto* again:

"Constant revolutionizing of production, uninterrupted disturbance of all social conditions, everlasting uncertainty and agitation distinguish the bourgeois epoch from all earlier ones. All fixed, fast-frozen relations, with their train of ancient and venerable prejudices and opinions, are swept away, all new-formed ones become antiquated before they can ossify. All that is solid melts into air, all that is holy is profaned, and man is at last compelled to face with sober senses his real conditions of life and his relations with his kind.

"The need of a constantly expanding market for its products chases the bourgeoisie over the whole surface of the globe. It must nestle everywhere, settle everywhere, establish connections everywhere.

"The bourgeoisie has, through its exploitation of the world market, given a cosmopolitan character to production and consumption in every country. To the great chagrin of reactionaries, it has drawn from under the feet of industry the national ground on which it stood. All old-established national industries have been destroyed or are daily being destroyed. They are dislodged by new industries whose introduction becomes a life-and-death question for all civilized nations, by industries that no longer work up indigenous raw material, but raw material drawn from the remotest zones; industries whose products are consumed, not only at home, but in every quarter of the globe. In place of the old wants, satisfied by the production of the country, we find new wants, requiring for their satisfaction the products of distant lands and

climes. In place of the old local and national seclusion
and self-sufficiency, we have intercourse in every direction,
universal inter-dependence of nations. And as in material,
so also in intellectual production. The intellectual crea-
tions of individual nations become common property.
National onesidedness and narrow-mindedness become
more and more impossible, and from the numerous
national and local literatures there arises a world litera-
ture."

But that world literature is a weakling child, prevented
from natural growth by the very conditions of capitalist
production which gave it birth. Race and national
hatreds, class enmity, the forcible prevention of the
national development of weak nations by strong, even
sex bias and sex antagonism, the opposition between
town and country, the ever-widening division between
mental and physical labour that is the result of the mass
production of commodities—all these things, arising from
the contradictions of capitalist society, are fetters on the
growth of a world literature. It follows then, that the
solution to the difficulties of the novelist, the solution
which can alone restore the epic character of reality to
his art form, is a revolutionary one, one that recognizes
the truth of our modern society.

CHAPTER V

THE NOVEL AS EPIC

IT is the main argument of this essay that the novel is the most important gift of bourgeois, or capitalist, civilisation to the world's imaginative culture. The novel is its great adventure, its discovery of man. It may be objected that capitalism has also given us the cinema, and this is true, but only in a technical sense, for it has proved so far unable to develop it as an art. The drama, music, painting and sculpture have all been developed by modern society, either for better or for worse, but all these arts had already gone through a long period of growth, as long almost as civilization itself, and their main problems were solved. With the novel, only one problem, the simplest one of all, that of telling a story, had been solved by the past.

Yet the novelists did not start off altogether from scratch. They had a certain amount of accumulated experience, an experience we can still use with profit to-day. As the Middle Ages drew to their close the trading communities of Italy and England produced the first tellers of tales in the modern manner, in which the characters of men and women, the way they did things, began to matter almost as much as what they did. Chaucer and Boccaccio first showed the most important feature of the novelist, a curiosity about men and women. Perhaps you can feel it a little in Malory, but he was writing almost a century later than Chaucer, and though his medium was prose, one feels that he has fallen a long way behind the poet. True, he was writing in the midst of a society in the full anarchy of decay, but you will find truer Englishmen and women (and sometimes better prose) in the Paston letters than in Malory.

Malory's knights and ladies, his Round Table and his mystic Grael, his killings and his bawdrie, have all the elements of that most pernicious form of bourgeois literature, Romanticism. I will not allow Malory to the Middle Ages any more than Scott or Chateaubriand. He tells his tale as well as Scott and his sentiment is seldom so nauseating as Chateaubriand's, but he remains the first great escapist, a man seeking refuge from a present both fearful and repellent in an idealized past. He abandoned realism, or rather, it never existed for him, Chaucer might never have lived, and if Malory ever read the *Canterbury Tales* he no doubt considered them unpleasantly vulgar. In a sense, Euphues and Arcadia are part of his romantic tradition, as was the *Faery Queen*. They have their virtues as poetry, or as imaginative prose, but they held back the English imagination from developing in fiction. Perhaps that was no great matter. Dramatic poetry took all the best of our national genius at that time, and the Elizabethan age, though it produced some glorious pub stories and rogues' tales in defiance of the Euphues tradition, did not noticeably advance the novel.

Nor did the seventeenth century. But here I think there is a point worth making. H. G. Wells, in his autobiography, lets slip a very profound piece of self-criticism. "Exhaustive character-study," he writes, "is an adult occupation, a philosophical occupation. So much of my life has been a prolonged and enlarged adolescence, an encounter with the world in general, that the observation of character began to play a leading part in it only in my latter years. It was necessary for me to reconstruct the frame in which individual lives as a whole had to be lived, before I could concentrate upon any of the individual problems of fitting them into this frame."

It is true that novel-writing is a philosophical occupation. The great novels of the world, *Don Quixote, Gargantua and Pantagruel, Robinson Crusoe, Jonathan Wild, Jacques Le Fataliste, Le Rouge et Le Noir, War and Peace, L'Education Sentimentale, Wuthering Heights, The Way of All Flesh,* are great precisely because they have this quality of thought behind them, because they are highly imaginative, inspired, if you like, commentaries on life. It is this quality which distinguishes the first-rate from the second-rate in fiction. It is true that there are philosophers who have lamentably failed to write novels, but no novelist has ever been able to create without possessing that ability for generalization about his characters which is the result of a philosophical attitude to life.

The seventeenth century produced no great novels, but it did produce the philosophers who made possible the triumphs of the following century. Somehow I cannot but feel that the eighteenth remains the supreme period in English fiction because it follows so closely upon the supreme period in English philosophy. English philosophy was the creation of the bourgeois revolution in our country, and it was profoundly materialist. "Materialism is the true son of Great Britain," writes Marx. "It was the English schoolman, Duns Scotus, who asked 'whether matter could not think.' " Berkeley, the first English idealist, only inverted Locke's sensualist philosophy, as Sterne only sentimentalized the materialism of Rabelais and the imaginative power of Cervantes.

Rabelais and Cervantes, the real founders of the novel, were more fortunate than their successors in that they did not live in the new society of which they were the heralds. They were men of the transition period, children of the revolutionary storms which broke up mediaeval feudalism, and they were inspired by the greatest flow of new ideas, the most exciting rebirth that man has ever known in his history (leaving aside the vexed question of whether or not we are to-day again entering on such a period).

Their two works are still to this day unchallenged for vigour of life, for force of imagination and for richness of language. They stood between two worlds. They were able to mock and to flay the vices of the old world, but they by no means uncritically accepted the new. The same is true of Shakespeare, and, indeed, of all the great figures of the Renaissance. Man has lost in stature since then what he has gained in mastery over the brave new world which they saw beginning to open before their delighted but not uncritical eyes.

Rabelais asserts the independence of that pathetic, curious and delightful instrument of life, the human body, and gives a new war-cry to the mind within that body, the mind which was just discovering life anew, "Do what you will!" He wrought a revolution in language no less astonishing than in thought, as a study of any competent historical grammar of the French language will tell us. Here again is a point to bear in mind—the immense significance of the writer in the revolutionizing of language. After the Renaissance the next great flow of life into the French language came from the romantic movement which was the child of the Great Revolution. The same is roughly true of our own language.

In Cervantes the revolutionary nature of his work is more implicit than explicit. The drama of his view of life expresses itself in the relation between his two chief characters and again in the relation of Quixote and Sancho to the world outside them. In this way his novel marks a step forward from Rabelais, but between them these two forged for the novelist every weapon that he needed. Rabelais gave him humour and the poetry of language, Cervantes gave him irony and the poetry of feeling. They were universal geniuses and no work equal in stature to theirs has since been written in that variegated prose fiction which we call the novel.

It is worth while to note that both were men of action

as well as novelists, that both suffered persecution, and
that neither of them would have known what Mr. David
Garnett meant if he had been able to talk to them about
a "pure artist." If they had managed at last to understand
that curious and contradictory phrase each would have
hugged it, after his own fashion, to his bosom, and then
unburdened himself, the one obscenely and happily, the
other gravely and ironically, upon such a peculiar and
perverted concept.

The novelists, the epic writers of the new society, had
therefore a great heritage on which to draw. How did
they acquit themselves of their task? In our own country,
for a half century or so, with honour, even though they
never achieved the heights which the French and Spanish
giants had conquered. The novel was a weapon, not in
the crude sense of being a political pamphlet, but in the
period of its birth and first healthy growth it was the
weapon by which the best, most imaginative representa-
tives of the bourgeoisie examined the new man and
woman and the society in which they lived. That is the
all-important fact about the eighteenth century writers.
They did not shrink from man, they believed in him,
believed in his ability to master the world, while they
were not for a moment blind to the cruelty and injustice
of this world of which their heroes were so much a part.

Fielding has been blamed because he introduced
"sermons" into his novels, but if the sermons were all
removed, the social criticism would be there just the
same, implicit in his story, and we should have lost some
of the best essays in the English language. Better to leave
the essays and accept the sad truth that Fielding, having
lived before Flaubert and the Goncourt brothers, not to
mention Henry James, really did not know that there
were certain rules in polite literary society which have to
be observed in the writing of a novel. He was the first
Englishman to understand that the job of a novelist was

to tell the truth about life as he saw it, and he told it in his own way. In *Jonathan Wild* he told it as it has never been told before or since, as even Swift never succeeded in telling it, with a fierce and brutal anger which lives because it is human anger awakened by the degradation of human life.

Fielding has been criticized, notably by Mr. David Garnett in his essay in *The English Novelists*, for lack of imagination expressed in a certain brutality towards suffering. It is true that there were some intimate depths of the human heart which found no expression in his work, he was an objective rather than a subjective writer, and if this limitation is at times a hindrance to his observation, it would be fair to say that the subjectivists, Richardson, Sterne and Rousseau, have probably lost even more by their renunciation of the objective world, and have limited their vision still more severely.

But the accusation of brutality as a reproach to Fielding the novelist is inept as well as unjust. He lived in a brutal world, the world of conquering capitalism, the period when the English squire was crushing the English peasant out of existence, when the English adventurer was stealing the wealth of the Indies by means as horrible as they were (in the abstract sense) immoral, and when that accumulation of stolen wealth was being made in the country which was to make possible the Industrial Revolution. That strange genius, Warren Hastings, our English revenge on the East for Genghis Khan, was a child in Fielding's day. Walpole was the Prime Minister of his maturity. And the chapters of *Jonathan Wild* on the great man's share in the proper division of booty and "of hats" are the true reflection of his corrupt and plundering age. As well accuse Fielding of brutality as the author of *Lady into Fox* of being insensitive to the real life of his own age.*

* The "brutal" Fielding, it is worth remembering, instigated some of the most important reforms in the barbarous judicial system

There is a dualism in the writers of the eighteenth century, not only interesting but important. Defoe, Fielding and Smollett are concerned with a purely objective picture of the world. Their characters have little or no "inner life," and these authors spend no time on analysis either of feeling or of motive, for they are more concerned with describing "how" than "why." This does not exclude "why." Far from it. It is usually sufficiently clear to the reader why a character acts as he does, for the action flows from the character as we know it. In the famous case, for example, where Moll Flanders refrained from murdering the child whom she robbed, it seems clear enough why she refrained, perfectly in keeping with Moll's character as we know it. For Defoe the interesting thing is that she was satisfied with robbery and stopped short of child murder. That appears more interesting than "why." Dostoievsky, however, could have written a whole novel for us entirely around this (relatively) trivial incident, a novel entirely concerned with "why."

The eighteenth century developed a completely new kind of novel, the novel concerned only with the individual's motives and feelings, in which the general social picture hardly counts at all. Robinson Crusoe was a supreme affirmation of the individual, but he was an individual who lived entirely outside himself, the typical man of the new world in one sense, but not in another. Crusoe discovered that he alone could conquer the world. It was left to Sterne and to Rousseau to discover that the individual alone *was* the world. The same thing had happened in philosophy when Berkeley turned Locke's empiricism upside down and produced his philosophy of subjective idealism which admitted no reality outside our

of our country. He was also the first man to draw up a scheme for a civilized police force which should inspire public respect and affection rather than fear and hatred.

own consciousness. It was a revolutionary and far-reaching idea in fiction, this taking of the consciousness of the individual as the starting point of one's picture of the world. It early reached its logical conclusion when Restif de Bretonne dedicated his autobiographical novel *Monsieur Nicolas* to himself, but if it could sometimes be ridiculous, and if in the end it destroyed the novel, the new method could also be sublime.

The fact is that neither the view of Fielding on reality nor the view of Richardson and Sterne is a complete one. The exclusion of sentiment and analysis, the failure to see the subjective side of the individual, deprived the novel of imagination and fantasy, just as the centring of all action in the individual consciousness deprived it of its epic quality. Such a division in Cervantes was unthinkable. It was the creation of a fully-developed capitalist society which had completed the separation of the individual from society, just as in another two generations it was to begin the subdivision of individuals themselves in the completion of its minute and complex division of social labour.

The new school, however, with their disturbing discovery of "sensibility," were the forerunners of a revolution in the novel. Richardson, a little tearfully but none the less truly, disclosed the most intimate feelings of the human heart. Had he only possessed Fielding's steady vision of life and firm hold on reality nothing could have prevented him from becoming one of the world's greatest novelists. It is a vain thing to wish a writer had possessed qualities he most obviously did not have, but this time there is some justification for the silly regret, since Richardson's failings have inevitably if unjustly reduced him to the position of a museum piece, from being a living writer to an historical and literary "influence."

Sterne carried the retreat from reality even further. Richardson had only been concerned with the feelings of his characters, but he had retained, despite his correspondence form which he borrowed from France and his own domestic experience, the traditions of the story told in time. Sterne at a blow destroyed all this. "To be or not to be" might well be called the central problem of the hero's fate in *Tristram Shandy*, in a literal sense undreamed of by Hamlet, and so far as this reader is concerned he never could discover for certain whether the problem was adequately solved, despite the complications attending the physical process of Tristram Shandy's birth which are so amusingly described. Sterne murders time in his novel. Shall a novel tell a story? Yes, answer the school of relativists, it may tell a story if it can be a detective story in which the reader seeks for the clue to beginning, middle and end, is continually baffled, and then has it all explained to him later by the author, or, in extreme cases, by the author's friends in specially written commentaries.

Sterne had all the divine gifts of the greatest novelists: he had irony, fantasy, a delight in obscenity, a love of humanity, everything the fairies bring to the genius at birth, everything but one gift, the ability to set his characters to live in a real world. He liked to think of himself as the English Rabelais, he copied Cervantes in the creation of Uncle Toby and Trim, but he was not Rabelais and he was most certainly not Cervantes. These two were discoverers of a new world, they were at war with life as well as in love with life, but Sterne was only the garrulous eighteenth-century gentleman trying to reconcile himself with Aristocratic society. He is much more amusing and has much more genius than his remote descendant Swann, but it is the same impulse that created the two books. Sterne was the first author to destroy time, to introduce relativism into the novel, but he did it, not in the interests of a greater reality, but because he found it easier that way to talk about himself. What

greater reality, asks the idealist, can there be than oneself?
Why, the reality of those who don't like you and think
you rather an ass, of course, the reality of those who
thought Sterne a self-advertising obscenity and Proust a
pretentious social climber. But they were wrong? Yes,
they were wrong, though Sterne and Proust by trying so
desperately to prove them wrong diminished their own
value as *creative* artists.

The real revolutionary of the eighteenth century was,
strictly speaking, not a novelist at all, though he was one
of the greatest imaginative prose writers of all time.
Rousseau held the illusion, fostered by eighteenth century
French materialism, that education could change man.
Certainly this is not all illusion, and if man's social en-
vironment is favourable it may even be true, provided
man is also actively working to change himself. Rousseau's
theory led him to believe that the influence of nature is
one of the most powerful influences which can change
man's character for the better. It is a sad illusion, but in
cultivating that illusion Rousseau did a great service to
literature, for he brought back nature into art. Without
him we should never have known Egdon Heath, nor
Tolstoi's reapers, nor Conrad's Pacific.

The eighteenth century was the golden age of the novel.
The novel of this period did not have the high fantasy of
Cervantes and Rabelais, who showed how imagination
can transform reality by a daemon force, but it was not
afraid of man and spoke the truth about life with an
uncompromising courage. It had wit also, and humour,
and it compelled man to understand that the individual
had an inner life as well as an outer life. It discovered
nature for him and it roused him to consider, in the
work of Fielding, Swift, Voltaire, Diderot and Rousseau,
that all was not for the best in the best of all possible
worlds. It roused him not before it was time, because the
world of the eighteenth century was about to die in the

greatest revolutionary convulsion of all history. But one thing the century failed to do. It produced no novel which combined the humane realism of Fielding with the sensibility of Richardson, with Sterne's ironic wit and Rousseau's passionate love of nature. Nor was the nineteenth century to succeed any better, though in Balzac and Tolstoi it came nearer than ever before. Indeed, taken as a whole, the nineteenth century was one of retreat, a retreat which has ended in a panic rout in our own day.

CHAPTER VI

THE VICTORIAN RETREAT

In England the development of the novel came to a sudden halt half-way through the eighteenth century. It seemed as though the genius of the country, which had flowed so naturally into the new epic form, had for a time to find its outlet elsewhere and otherwise. The sentimentalities of Goldsmith and the artificial romanticism of Walpole are a painful descent from the achievements of Smollett, Fielding and Sterne. Such passion for life as there was in the new bourgeoisie sought expression in the religious movement started by John Wesley, while the commercialized aristocracy turned to France for their intellectual fare, or to the moral felicities of the *fin de siècle* poets. Much of our national genius was diverted also, fortunately for the country, into politics during the critical period of the American Revolution and after.

What had happened? The first half of the century had brought a literary movement only surpassed in our history by the Elizabethans, the second half brought stagnation and decline. The early eighteenth century had not been afraid to examine man as the new bourgeois society had created him. They had not always been particularly pleased with the creature, these poets, satirists and novelists, but they had faithfully recorded him as they found him. But now comes a fear of man, almost a hatred of him. He is no longer a cruel, cheerful, lusty, struggling, and human creature. He is a sinner to be saved. Wherein lies the secret of this fall from grace?

It is to be found in the development of the country itself, in the growing power of money that poisoned the relations between man and man, between man and woman, in the contrast of riches and poverty, in the heartless expropriation of the peasantry and the grim wretchedness of life in the new towns which were growing up to replace the old market centres and country seats. The American war had been fought and lost by the corrupt oligarchy who misruled the country in the name of the German King. India had been plundered to replace the losses of the war, while no one seemed to understand clearly that the foundation of the first democratic republic five thousand miles away across the Atlantic had changed the history of the world. No one, that is, save a few unknown pamphleteers and one or two rascally politicians.

When the English novelists began to look at man again and tell the epic of English life, so much had changed in the world that the novel was hardly the same thing at all. The instrument had been blunted as well as the vision of the artist. Scott, the first great novelist of this new industrial age, ran away from it altogether into the idealized and romanticized past. He was a revolutionary innovater in one sense, for he first made it clear that it is not enough to look at man, he must also be examined historically. He knew that man had a past as well as a present, and his astonishing and fertile genius attempted to make the synthesis which the eighteenth century had failed to produce, in which the novel should unite the poetry as well as the prose of life, in which the nature-love of Rousseau should be combined with the sensibility of Sterne and the vigour and amplitude of Fielding.

He failed, but it was a glorious failure, and the reasons are worth examination. It is popular to-day to deprecate Scott as a mere teller of skilfully contrived and intolerably sentimental stories. Mr. E. M. Forster sees him as that, but Balzac had a different view. Scott is the only novelist to whom Balzac acknowledges a real and deep debt, and with all respect to Mr. Forster, himself our only considerable contemporary novelist, I prefer the view taken by Balzac.

Why did Scott fail in his immense task? Because impenetrable blinkers obscured his vision. If the modern critic would here interject that this is exactly his opinion, I would answer that the blinkers are the same as those obscuring the vision of the modern critic, with the difference that Scott was a genius, even though blinkered. Scott was unable to see man as he is. His characters are not the real men and women of history, but rather his own idealizations of the early nineteenth century English upper middle-class and commercialized aristocracy. The difference between Scott's characters and the characters of Fielding lies precisely in this fact, that his men and women are idealizations while Fielding's are types.

It had become impossible for the novelist to see his people truly. Even Jane Austen, who almost succeeded, surrenders with every character. She is critical, ironical, analyses her people truly, shows that they and their problems are incapable of solution within their society, and then, tamely surrenders. This is their world of sheltered gentility, there is another outside, but its existence must never, never be recognized. It is almost now as though we are dealing with writers who have been castrated, not physically, but spiritually. To explain it by the puritanism of the new world, particularly the Victorian world, is not enough, for had it been at all possible a great writer would have broken down that puritanism (Byron did so in poetry a generation earlier). The difficulty was that the writer himself saw life in this way. He was incapable of a vision of man as he is, but only of a vision of man as he fitted the new industrial society.

Thackeray disliked the new bourgeoisie and showed his dislike plainly, in scorching satire. So did many a lesser writer, but they never dared to show again the whole man in his relations with the real world as the eighteenth century had shown him. It is not that the Victorians were afraid of sex. Far from it, in their own way, not always a very pleasant way, they could be frank enough about that question. When the worst has been said, Becky Sharp is not so different from the heroines of the Restoration comedy, though she is considerably more polite of speech.

The difficulty was that the Victorian writer could not discuss the real relations between men and women without tearing the veil off the real relations between man and man in society. This was the period of the workhouses, the hungry forties, the Chartist strikes, the Newport rising, the period when for the first time in English history since 1688 a change in the fundamental law of the country was carried through under threat of armed force. It was the period of the worship of money and success, the period of factory development when whole tracts of England's most beautiful country were transformed into a wilderness. It was a time of rapacious materialism in public and private life covered by the sickliest hypocritical cloak of idealism. If you told the truth about the Victorian family you could hardly avoid telling the truth about these other aspects also, including Victorian "goodness" and piety in general. Later in the century Samuel Butler, in one of the really great Victorian novels, did tell the truth. His book was published after his death and only won recognition in our own time.

It was not that the Victorians would not see honestly, so much as that they could not. It would be as foolish to blame them for the limitations imposed on them by their age as to ignore their very real achievement. They did revive the English novel, which after its first glorious triumph in the middle of the last century had almost died out. In Dickens they had a genius who restored to the novel its full epic character, whose teeming mind created stories, poems and people which have forever entered into the life of the English-speaking world. Some of his characters have assumed an almost proverbial existence, they have become part of our modern folk-lore, and that surely is the highest any author can achieve. He can only do it by genius, humanity and a feeling for the poetry of life.

But despite all this, Dickens, no more than his contemporaries, was master of his own age. His fantasy, his power of poetic evocation, coupled with his ability to invent endless incident, to portray his people as reflections of all sorts of common and endearing human weaknesses and virtues, won him his public. He was of his age, though he never dominated it. He has been attacked for not being an artist (whatever that may mean in this connection), for being a reader's rather than a writer's writer. So much the worse for the writer then. The same is said of Scott, who was the greatest outside influence on Balzac, the man who dominates the first half of the nineteenth century. Dickens was perhaps the strongest of all foreign influences on Tolstoi, the man who dominates the second half of the century.

Why did Scott not reach to the dominating position of Balzac, or Dickens attain the stature of Tolstoi? Why shall we always find something lacking in the heroes of Dickens and Scott? It was because they could not see through the surface respectability of their society to the progressive degradation of man going on beneath. Because they could not see this process, neither could they truly see the real glory of their contemporaries, the heroic character of their times. The Victorians were well enough aware of the shallowness of the standards of the triumphant middle class, and they could flay that shallowness as well as the next man, but they could not see the deeper processes of spiritual disintegration at work. They could not see the *baseness* of capitalist society.

The French realists of the nineteenth century were

superior to the British in this, as we shall see in the next chapter. They saw clearly, but they also lost their battle, with the one exception of Balzac, in the effort to dominate reality. In the reaction against Romanticism with its false values the French novelists reached a position severely and uncompromisingly critical of bourgeois society, a position made possible, even inevitable, by the greater sharpness of the struggle of classes in France, which made it difficult to retain any illusions. Unfortunately, this critical position became a negative one not only in the social sense, but also in the aesthetic sense. In the end it proved to be not a step to the salvation of the novel by leading to a deeper realism, but a step towards its further disintegration and eventually away from realism.

The English realists retained their illusions about society. They did so by making a compromise with romanticism, that Victorian whore with the mock-modestly averted glance. There is a strange paradox in the fate of the nineteenth century novelist. His predecessors had written frankly: frankly about the physical things of life, about the law, about morals, about property, about love and war. They had written mainly for a very small and highly educated public which considered it one of their class privileges to indulge the luxury of an enlightened and "philosophical" view of the realities of human existence.

Not so with the nineteenth century writer. He was to be tormented by his *public*, by that great mass of the semi-educated lower middle-class or self-educated working class. There are things you cannot say to the masses if you are a decent middle-class man. A judge who last year tried a case of obscenity against the author of a book on sex quite seriously pointed out that it is all right to describe the pleasures of love for a select public, but that when you write down certain things and make them accessible to any woman of the working class, it is altogether a different affair, calling for both censure and punishment. The nineteenth century English got over this difficulty by their veil of romance. The French took refuge in a dumb and sullen hatred for this public who made possible their existence as writer yet destroyed (as it seemed to them) their conscience as artists. The Russians, who were in a peculiar position, rather like that of the French in the eighteenth century, but with all the advantages of having the progress in the novel made by the other two countries behind them when they started, fared better and were neither forced into compromises nor driven off the field of battle.

It is one of the purposes of this book to try to show some of the difficulties of the novelist in portraying the soul of man. My belief is that this soul can only be adequately pictured by the epic style which is the real secret of the novel's success as an art form. Since Rabelais and Cervantes that epic style had been gradually going through a process of refinement and attrition till by the end of the nineteenth century there was very little of it left, and precious little of the novel, into the bargain. The appearance of the reader on the scene as a force almost as important as the writer, finished off the process. It might, of course, have saved it. It was the complete harmony between the rhapsodist and his audience which made the poetic epic, and clearly enough, if only some such similar harmony between writer and public could have been established, the novel would have developed rather than declined.

Dickens was bombarded with letters begging him to spare the life of Little Nell. Hardy, on the other hand, was abused and threatened with prosecution, while across the Channel, where there was considerable literary integrity and artistic courage, Flaubert, the Goncourts and Zola all had to face criminal prosecution. These were the two extremes between which the shipwreck of the novel seemed inevitable. "Society," by which we mean the ruling class, could not allow the moral perversion of "the public," though it was itself perverting it morally and spiritually with all the immense resources at its command. The author who would continue the grand tradition of the English novel was no longer able to sit apart and observe the life of the nation, to be angry, ironical, pitiful and cruel as occasion demanded. This had been the advantage of the eighteenth-century writer, that there was no chance of any but the smallest number of his characters, the wealthy and privileged ones, reading his books. You could be as truthful as you liked about these, for they felt themselves socially secure and had enough of a humane tradition of letters to be able to stand the novelist's scorn without flinching.

But how was it with Dickens? His London read his books. He and his London were one. If he had been able to see the life of Seven Dials as it really was, he would have found the picture overwhelmingly horrible, his name would have become a battle-ground, he might even have found the task too great for him and turned away in loathing and disgust from the city he loved. He chose the easier method of sentimentalizing reality. In France the conflict of realism and romanticism was solved along different lines, apparently more honest, though in the end they bore no more fruit. So Dickens, who has some right to be considered the last great English novelist in the grand style, nevertheless failed when judged by the highest standards of his craft. He had fantasy, but not poetry; humour, but not irony; sentiment, but not feeling; he gave a picture of his age, but he did not express his age; he compromised with reality but he did not create a new romanticism.

Apart from Dickens, who has something of the universal genius, the novel in Victorian times disintegrates as it becomes more specialized. In place of *Tom Jones* we have a humorous novel, an adventure novel, a novel of the open road, a crime novel, and so on. Where Cervantes could combine imagination and poetry with humour and fantasy, we now have the purely imaginative and poetic novel, the purely humorous and fantastic. Certainly, the attempt finally to divide the subjective from the objective attitude to life, already clear in the eighteenth century, is suspended till our day, the period of the crisis of the individual. On the whole, however, the nineteenth century is a period of the break-up of the traditional form. Mr. Forster's approach to the novel in his book *Aspects of the Novel*, is a reflection of this, with its division into novels of "story," novels of "fantasy," novels of "prophecy." The division is not altogether conscious, but it is there none the less.

In fact, it is the conditions of nineteenth century capitalism which create and enforce this artificial division, which has nothing to do with the character of the novel itself. Where, it will be objected, are the conditions of nineteenth-century capitalism in such a purely "prophetic" novel as Emily Brontë's *Wuthering Heights*? Surely no materialist view could explain this book? What relation has it to the nineteenth or any other century? It is beyond time and space, immortal, primeval and elemental as the passion which gives the book its life. It is the novel become pure poetry.

Wuthering Heights is certainly the novel become poetry, it is beyond all doubt one of the most extraordinary books which human genius has ever produced, yet it is these things only because it is a cry of despairing agony wrung from Emily by life itself. The life of mid-Victorian England, experienced by a girl of passion and imagination imprisoned in the windswept parsonage on the moors of the West Riding, produced this book. Charlotte expressed the thwarted, lonely lives of these girls in the sublimated love of Rochester and Jane Eyre, in the burning story of

Lucy Snowe in *Vilette*. Emily could not be satisfied with this. Her love must triumph, and in the violent, horror-laden atmosphere of the stone farmhouse on the moors, it did triumph. Catherine and Heathcliffe are the revenge of love against the nineteenth century.

"My fingers closed on the fingers of a little, ice-cold hand! The intense horror of nightmare came over me: I tried to draw back my arm, but the hand clung to it, and a most melancholy voice sobbed, 'Let me in—let me in!' 'Who are you?' I asked, struggling, meanwhile, to disengage myself. 'Catherine Linton' it replied shiveringly. . . . 'I'm come home; I'd lost my way on the moor!' As it spoke, I discerned, obscurely, a child's face looking through the window. Terror made me cruel; and, finding it useless to attempt shaking the creature off, I pulled its wrist onto the broken pane, and rubbed it to and fro till the blood ran down and soaked the bedclothes: still it wailed, 'Let me in!' and maintained its tenacious grip, almost maddening me with fear. 'How can I!' I said at length. 'Let *me* go, if you want me to let you in!' The fingers relaxed, I snatched mine through the hole, hurriedly piled the books up in a pyramid against it, and stopped my ears to exclude the lamentable prayer. I seemed to keep them closed above a quarter of an hour; yet, the instant I listened again, there was the doleful cry moaning on! 'Begone!' I shouted, 'I'll never let you in, not if you beg for twenty years.' 'It is twenty years,' mourned the voice: 'twenty years. I've been a waif for twenty years!'"

It is the most terrible passage in English literature in the nineteenth century, but it is not, even in the intensity which gives it such life, outside of space and time. For the words of agony are wrung from Emily by her own time and no other age could have tortured her so sharply, twisted the words of aching, awful suffering out of her in accents of such terrifying force. Through the book, with the grotesque and horrid echo of a chorus, runs the complaint of the farm-hand Joseph, the canting, joyless, hating and hateful symbol of the obscene morality of his age, as though the prison walls themselves are endowed with voice to mock and spurn the prisoner.

The present writer was born and brought up less than a dozen miles from Haworth parsonage, in a society that had not fundamentally changed since the days of the three sisters, where the freaks of Bramwell were still remembered, and he sees nothing in Emily's novel that is "pure" poetry in the sense in which that odd phrase is used by those who love it so. It is the most violent and frightful cry of human suffering which even Victorian England ever tore from a human being.

Indeed, the three greatest books of the age were all such cries of suffering. *Wuthering Heights*, *Jude the Obscure*, and *The Way of All Flesh*, were the manifestos of English genius that a full human life in a capitalist society was impossible of attainment. The love of woman for man was a waif driven shrieking on to the cold moors, the love of man for his children brought them to that awful end in the Oxford lodging-house, the end the farmer gives to his pigs, while honesty, intelligence and simplicity bring your nineteenth-century hero to prison whence he can only be ransomed and given freedom by the unexpected gift of Aunt Alethea's £70,000 in North-Western Railway shares. These three books are a long way from Dickens, they belong indeed to another world from that of Dickens, and they are, in a sense, only mighty fragments, mutilated statues. In them, however, the real tradition of the novel is kept alive, and the writer of the future will acknowledge them as his inspiration when he attempts the task of conquering reality, that ceaseless creative war in which Dickens hauled down the battle flag to replace it by a blameless white flag of sentimental compromise.

CHAPTER VII

THE PROMETHEANS

MARX concluded one of his articles in the *New York Tribune* during 1854 with a reference to the Victorian realists: "The present brilliant school of novelists in England, whose graphic and eloquent descriptions have revealed more political and social truths to the world than have all the politicians, publicists and moralists added together, has pictured all sections of the middle class, beginning with the 'respectable' rentier and owner of government stocks, who looks down on all kinds of 'business' as being vulgar, and finishing with the small shopkeeper and lawyer's clerk. How have they been described by Dickens, Thackeray, Charlotte Brontë and Mrs. Gaskell? As full of self-conceit, prudishness, petty tyranny and ignorance. And the civilized world has confirmed their verdict in a damning epigram which it has pinned on that class, that it is servile to its social superiors and despotic to its inferiors."

About the same time as these words appeared in the New York paper, Flaubert in physical agony was writing to his friend Louis Bouilhet: "Laxatives, purgatives, derivatives, leeches, fever, diarrhoea, three nights without any sleep, a gigantic annoyance at the bourgeois, etc., etc. That's my week, dear sir." English and French novelists were alike faced with the same problem, that of giving artistic form and expression to a society which they could not accept. In England they only succeeded in the end by a kind of compromise with reality, but the whole history of France made such a compromise impossible in that country. No country of the modern world had passed through such terrific struggles as France, with her great revolution followed by twenty years of wars in which French armies marched and counter-marched across the feudal states of Europe till the final catastrophe of 1814.

Napoleon was the last great world-conqueror, but he was also the first bourgeois emperor. France was only able to support that vast war-machine because in those years she began to catch up her rival England, to develop her industries, to introduce power machinery on a large scale, to create a great new internal market from her liberated peasantry. When the process was completed, a generation after Napoleon's fall, you had the strange paradox that a completely new France, a France in which money spoke the last word, a France of bankers, traders and industrialists, was being ruled by the feudal aristocracy whom the revolution had apparently smashed into fragments. Yet the heroic tradition of this new France with its old rulers remained essentially revolutionary, on the one hand the Jacobin of '93, on the other the soldier of Napoleon.

Balzac, the great genius of the century, consciously set himself the task of writing "the natural history" of this society, Balzac who was himself a monarchist, a legitimist and a Catholic. His *Comédie Humaine*, that encyclopaedic study of human life, was a revolutionary picture of his age, revolutionary, not because of the intention of its author, but because of the truth with which the inner life of his time is described. Engels, in his letter to the English novelist, Margaret Harkness, has emphasized the *truth* of Balzac's realist method: "Balzac, whom I consider a far greater master of realism than all the Zolas, *passés, présents et à venir*, in his *Comédie Humaine* gives us a most wonderfully realistic history of French society, describing in chronicle fashion, almost year by year, from 1816 to 1848, the progressive inroads of the rising bourgeoisie upon the society of nobles that reconstituted itself after 1815, and that set up again as far as it could the standard of *la vieille politesse française*. He describes how the last remnants of this, to him, model society, gradually succumbed before the intrusion of the vulgar, moneyed upstart, or were corrupted by him, how the grande dame, whose conjugal infidelities were but a mode of asserting herself, in perfect accordance with the way she had been disposed of in marriage, gave way to the bourgeois who gains her husband for cash or customers; and around this central picture he groups a complete history of French society, from which, even in economic details, for instance, the rearrangement of real and personal property after the Revolution, I have learnt more than from all the professed historians, economists and statisticians of the period together. Well, Balzac was politically a legitimist; his great work is a constant elegy unto the irreparable decay of good society; his sympathy is with the class that is doomed to extinction. But for all that his satire is never more cutting, his irony more biting than when he sets in motion the very men and women with whom he sympathizes most deeply—the nobles. And the only men of whom he speaks with undisguised admiration are his bitterest political antagonists, the Republican heroes of the Cloitre-Saint-Merri, the men who at that time (1830–36), were indeed the representatives of the popular masses. That Balzac was thus compelled to go against his own class sympathies and political prejudices, that he *saw* the necessity of the downfall of his favourite nobles and described them as people deserving no better fate; that he saw the real men of the future where, for the time being, they alone could be found—that I consider one of the greatest triumphs of Realism, one of the greatest features in old Balzac."

Balzac has himself explained in the Preface to the *Comédie* that he saw man as the product of society, saw him in his natural environment, and that he felt the same desire to study him scientifically as the great naturalists feel who study the animal world. His political and religious views were those of the old feudal France, but this attitude to man, this conception of the human comedy, was the product of the Revolution, of the Jacobins who so ruthlessly smashed the social fetters on French society, of the marching soldiers who brought the monarchies of Europe to their knees before the leadership of Napoleon. Balzac, indeed, was France's literary Napoleon, for he destroyed feudal ideas in literature, as thoroughly as the great soldier destroyed the feudal system in politics. In Restoration France criticism of capitalist society, of the new capitalist social relations, was concealed under the mediaeval disguise of romanticism. The extravagances of the Romantics in their personal lives, quite as much as their extravagances in art, were a protest against the present as well as an escape from it. Balzac neither protested nor escaped. He had all the imagination, the poetry and even the mysticism of the Romantics, but he rose above them and showed the way to a new literature by his realist attack on the present. He was able to conceive the reality of contemporary life imaginatively, to conceive it almost on the scale on which Rabelais and Cervantes had conceived it. It was his fortune, however, to have lived in the early part of the century, when the force and fire of that immense outburst of national energy which made the Revolution and the Napoleonic epic, was still able to make itself felt in the literary movement of the thirties and early forties.

It was a long way from Balzac to the Flaubert whose dominant passion was hatred and disgust of the bourgeoisie, who signed his letters "Bourgeoisophobus" and suffered such physical and mental agony in the long years of creative work he gave to a single novel on the life of this hated and despised class. Balzac was consciously proud of his political views, of his royalism and catholicism. The Goncourt brothers wrote in their *Diary* that their disillusionment in the good faith of politicians of all sorts brought them, in the end, to "a disgust in every belief, a toleration for any kind of power, an indifference towards political passion which I find in all my literary friends, in Flaubert as well as myself. You can see that one should die for no cause, that one should live with any government there is, no matter what one's antipathy to it, and believe in nothing but art, confess no faith but literature."

So many writers since, of considerably less talent than the two Goncourts and whose names cannot even be mentioned in the same breath with Flaubert, have professed (and still profess) a similar outlook, that it is worth our while to seek the origin of this apparent disillusionment and detachment from life. I say "apparent" because in Flaubert's case at least (he was a great writer) there was no detachment, but a bitter battle to the death with that bourgeois society he hated so violently.

The Goncourts knew Balzac personally, their diaries are full of anecdotes about that vital and Rabelaisian genius. Flaubert, like themselves, also overlapped him in his creative work. Whence comes the great difference between the master and the disciples, a difference not in time but in outlook that divides them like a gulf? The energy engendered by the Revolution and its heroic aftermath had died out by the advent of Flaubert's generation. The bitter struggle of classes and the real predatory character of capitalist society had become so clear, that they aroused only disgust; whereas Balzac, still inspired by the creative force that built this society, sought only for understanding.

The democratic and Jacobin ideals of '93, in the mouths of the liberal politicians of the nineteenth century had become intolerable and monstrous platitudes. The real *levelling* character of capitalism was becoming apparent, its denial of human values, its philosophy of numbers that covered its cash estimate for all things human and divine. The old aristocracy whose corruption Balzac had drawn in such masterly fashion was nothing but a decayed shadow of its old self, an obscene ghost muttering and grumbling in the forgotten drawing-rooms of provincial country-houses, or else indistinguishable from the new nobility of hard cash. Socialism, only known to Flaubert and his friends in its Utopian form, seemed to them as stupid and unreal as the worst extravagances of the liberal politicians who daily in word and deed betrayed their great ancestors. (That Flaubert considered them great ancestors there is plenty of evidence: "Marat is my man," he writes in one letter.) Socialism was only another form of the general levelling of all values which so revolted them, and rendered the more disgusting because of its sentimental idealizing (it seemed to them) of the uneducated mob.

The period of 1848 saw the end of many illusions. Who after that bitter experience would ever again believe that fine words could butter parsnips? The June days, in which the Paris workers took the spinners of phrases at their word and fought in arms for liberty, equality and fraternity, were the writing on the wall. Flaubert was a novelist, not a student of the social history and economic machinery of mankind, and to him the June days merely proved that flirting with empty slogans roused dark forces who were a threat to the very existence of civilized society. The dictatorship of the blackguard Louis Napoleon which followed was just a dictatorship of blackguards, the apotheosis of the bourgeois, and all that could be expected from the follies of preceding years. So the *Education Sentimentale* is a bitter and mercilessly ironical picture of the end of all the fine illusions of the liberal bourgeoisie, illusions which the red flag and rifle shots of June, 1848, shattered for ever. After that the vulgarity of the Empire.

Nothing would be the same again and one could resign oneself to the long process of social decay and destruction of civilization by this stupid and miserly bourgeoisie, with its wars, its narrow nationalism and its bestial greed.

It might be thought that between Flaubert's theory of god-like objectivity of the artist and Balzac's theory of the natural history of social man there is no great difference. In fact, there is all the difference in the world. Balzac's scientific views were possibly naïve and incorrect, but in his view of life he was truly realist. He looked at human society historically, as something struggling and developing through its struggles. In Flaubert life becomes frozen and static. After 1848 you could not observe and express life in its development because that development was too painful, the contradictions were too glaring. So life became for him a frozen lake. "What appears beautiful to me," he writes to his mistress, "what I should like to do, would be a book about nothing, a book without any attachment to the external world, which would support itself by the inner strength of its style, just as the world supports itself in the air without being held up, a book which would be almost without a subject, or in which the subject would be almost invisible, if that is possible. The most beautiful books are those with the least matter. The nearer the expression comes to the thought, the more the word clings to it and then disappears, the more beautiful it is."

Once this view was accepted the way was clear for the new "realism" which took the slice of life and described it minutely and objectively. But life, of course, proved too restive a creature to slice up artistically, so the novelist grew finicking about the choosing of his slice, demanding that it be cut off such a refined portion of life's anatomy that in the end he came to describe little more interesting than the suburban street, or the Mayfair party. Revolting against the narrow view imposed on their vision by this theory, others drew their inspiration from Freud and Dostoievsky in order to give us the poetic picture of their own stream of consciousness. So in the end the novel has died away into two tendencies whose opposition has as little about it that is important to us as the mediaeval battles of the schoolmen.

Flaubert, however, was an honest man and a great artist. If his successors were content to avoid the task of mastering the reality of their age and substitute the "slice of life" or the subjective stream of consciousness, he was not prepared to make any such easy surrender. His letters are the confession of a most frightful struggle with a life, a reality, that had become loathsome to him, but which nevertheless must be mastered and given artistic expression. No man has ever raged against the bourgeoisie with the hatred of Flaubert. "I would drown humanity in my vomit," he writes, and he does not mean humanity as a whole, but only the capitalist society of nineteenth century Europe, immediately after the Paris Commune of 1871.

Letter after letter describes his struggle to find expression. He takes two months to write the tavern scene for *Madame Bovary*, the duration of which in the novel itself is only three hours. Over and over again he mentions that in the last month he has written some twenty pages. Can this be explained simply by his devotion to the perfect phrase, to the exact word? Is it an artist's conscience which will be satisfied with nothing less than perfection in style? Hardly that. He himself says that the works in which the greatest attention has been paid to style and form are mostly second-rate, and in one place declares outright that he is not sure if it is possible to find a criterion for perfection in style. When he writes of the great authors of the world, it is enviously: "They had no need to strive for style, they are strong in spite of all faults and because of them; but we, the minor ones, only count by our perfection of execution. . . . I will venture a suggestion here I would not dare to make anywhere else: it is that the very great often write very badly and so much the better for them. We mustn't look for the art of form in them, but in the second-raters like Horace and La Bruyère."

Yet Flaubert did not live in physical and mental agony, shut up in his country home among people he despised, because he was a second-rate artist seeking formal perfection. No, he was a great and honest artist striving to express a world and a life he hated and his whole artistic theory was the result of the compromise enforced on him in that struggle. "Art must in no way be confused with the artist. All the worse for him if he does not love red, green or yellow, all colours are beautiful, and his job is to paint them. . . . Look at the leaves for themselves; to understand nature one must be calm as nature." Or again, the famous letter in which he sums up his credo: "The author in his work must be like God in the universe, present everywhere and visible nowhere; art being a second nature, the creator of this nature must act by similar methods; in each atom, in every aspect, there must be felt a hidden and infinite impassibility."

Flaubert himself failed utterly to live up to his precepts. Such a god feels neither love nor hate. Flaubert's whole life was animated by hate, a holy hatred of his age which was a kind of inverted love for man deceived, tormented and debased by a society whose only criterion of value was property. He gave his view of that society at last in the irony of *Bouvard and Pécuchet*, a novel which arose out of his scheme for a *Dictionary of Accepted Ideas* in which you were to find "in alphabetical order on every possible subject everything which you need to say in society to be accepted as a respectable and nice fellow."

Flaubert, like Dickens, was a great writer faced with the problem of giving a true picture of a society whose very premises were rapidly becoming a denial of the standards of humanism once looked on as our common heritage. Dickens solved his problem by the compromise of sentimental romanticism. English conditions made it inevitable for him. Flaubert, who lived in the France of June, 1848, of the Third Empire, the Franco-Prussian War and the Commune, had to take another road. Not only his own temperament, his uncompromising honesty, forbade the path of sentimentality (how easy that would have been for a less great man, Daudet was to show), but the harsher reality of French life irrevocably closed that path for him. He stood apart from the struggle, with infinite pain created for himself an unreal objectivity, and tried to isolate by means of a purely formal approach, certain aspects of life. Poor Flaubert, who suffered more terribly than any writer of his time in his effort to create a picture of life, who more than any man felt the real pulse of his age, yet could not express it, this man of deep passion and intense hatred, has suffered the sad fate of becoming that colourless thing, the highbrow's example of the "pure artist." Why we should admire a "pure artist" more than a "pure woman" is one of the mysteries of the age. Why not just an artist, and a woman? They are both interesting and they both suffer, but not in order to be beautiful.

There was one contemporary of Flaubert's who went through the same agony of creation, who tormented himself for weeks in order to find the precise words to express the reality he was determined to dominate and refashion in his mind. This other artist wrote and re-wrote, fashioned and re-fashioned, loved and hated with an even greater intensity and finally gave the world the mighty fragments created by his genius. His name was Karl Marx and he successfully solved the problem which had broken every other of his contemporaries, the problem of understanding completely the world of the nineteenth century and the historical development of capitalist society.

"From form is born the idea," Flaubert told Gautier, who regarded these words as being "the supreme formula" of this school of "objective" realism, worthy to be carved on walls. Content determines form, was the view of Marx, but between the two there is an inner relationship, a unity, an indissoluble connection. Flaubert's ideal was to write a book "about nothing," a work of pure formalism, in which the logical was torn apart from the factual and historical. In its extremest form, as developed by Edmond de Goncourt, Huysmans and others, this became a pure subjectivism, which converted the object into the passive material of the subject, the novelist, who in turn was reduced to a mere photographer.

Lafargue, Marx's son-in-law and a keen critic of the French realists, has contrasted the two methods: "Marx did not merely see the surface, but penetrated beneath, examined the component parts in their reciprocity and mutual interaction. He isolated each of these parts and traced the history of its growth. After that he approached the thing and its environment and observed the action of the latter upon the former, and the reverse. He then returned to the birth of the object, to its changes, evolutions and revolutions and went into its uttermost activities. He did not see before him a separate thing for itself and in itself having no connection with its environment, but a whole complicated and eternally moving world. And Marx strove to represent the life of that world in its various and constantly changing actions and reactions. The writers of the school of Flaubert and Goncourt complain of the difficulties the artist encounters in trying to reproduce what he sees. But they only try to represent the surface, only the impression they receive. Their literary work is child's play in comparison with that of Marx. An unusual strength of mind was called for in order to understand so profoundly the phenomenon of reality, and the art needed to transmit what he saw and wished to say was no less."

Lafargue rightly estimates the creative method of Marx, and correctly shows the deficiencies of Flaubert's method, though he does not understand that Flaubert himself in his heart of hearts was aware of its deficiencies. Neither does Lafargue realize the forces which drove Flaubert and the Goncourt brothers to adopt their artistic method. The diary has some interesting light to throw on this last point. In 1855, Edmond writes that "every four· or five hundred years barbarism is necessary to revitalize the world. The world would die of civilization. Formerly in Europe whenever the old population of some pleasant country had become suitably affected with anaemia, there fell on their backs from the North, a lot of fellows six feet tall who remade the race. Now there are no more barbarians in Europe and it is the workers who will accomplish this task. We shall call it the social revolution."

In the midst of the Commune he remembered this prophecy. "What is happening," he wrote, "is the complete conquest of France by the working-class population, and the enslavement of noble, bourgeois and peasant beneath its despotism. The government is slipping out of the hands of the possessing classes into the hands of those with no possessions, from the hands of those who have a material interest in the preservation of society, into the hands of those who have no interest in order, stability and conservatism. After all, perhaps in the great law of change of things here below, the workers, as I said some years ago, take the place of the barbarians in ancient society, the part of convulsive agents of destruction and dissolution."

Neither Flaubert nor the Goncourts saw the working class as anything but a purely destructive agent. They did not suffer from any illusions about bourgeois society, they hated its greed, its narrow nationalism, its lack of values, its general levelling tendency and degradation of man, but they saw no alternative to this society, and here is the fundamental weakness of their work. After Flaubert, critical realism could progress no further, for his tremendous labours had exhausted the method. Either the novelist must again see society in movement, as Balzac had done, or he must turn into himself, become completely subjective, deny space and time, break up the whole epic structure. There was also a further difficulty, one that had been growing for more than a hundred years, and was now reaching its acutest tension, the difficulty of a unified outlook on life, of the ability to deal with human character at all.

The great novelists of the Renaissance had not felt this difficulty. For them humanism had given direction to their ideas and inspired their work. The Renaissance produced its great philosophers, though at the end of the period rather than the beginning, in Spinoza, Descartes and Bacon. Certainly, even here the main division in human thought is apparent in the conflict of Descartes and Spinoza, but in the seventeenth and eighteenth centuries it was not yet so violent as to destroy all philosophic unity. The English and French realist novelists on the whole had a similar view of life, their work in consequence gains in completeness and force. In the nineteenth century, however, the period when all the violent contradictions of the capitalist social system became clear, when wars and revolutions destroy the last feudal strongholds in Europe and the modern nations are formed, there is no longer any philosophical unity. Kant and Hegel have so developed idealism that it temporarily overwhelms the realist, materialist philosophies. The century is one without a unified view of human life, so that it becomes more and more difficult for the novelist to work except in a minor, specialized way, by isolating some fragment of life

or of individual consciousness. Flaubert's letters are full
of this feeling, and he describes his vain efforts to master
the philosophers, his rifling of the works of Kant, Hegel,
Descartes, Hume and the rest. All the time he feels the
desire to get back to Spinoza, as the Goncourts felt the
desire to get back to the dialectic thought of Diderot.
But in the end they give up the search for a philosophical
basis as being impossible of fulfilment in the contemporary
world.

It is the tragedy of Flaubert and his school that they
so continually and acutely felt their own insufficiency,
were so conscious of the great superiority of the masters
of the past, Rabelais, Cervantes, Diderot and Balzac.
Sometimes they almost blundered on the reason for this,
and there is a passage on Balzac in the Goncourt diary
which comes so close to the truth and is so significant for
the writer to-day, that it will perfectly sum up the argu-
ment of this chapter.

"I have just re-read Balzac's *Peasants*. Nobody has ever
called Balzac a statesman, yet he was probably the
greatest statesman of our time, the only one to get to the
bottom of our sickness, the only one who saw from on
high the disintegration of France since 1789, the manners
beneath the laws, the facts behind the words, the anarchy
of unbridled interests beneath the apparent order, the
abuses replaced by influences, equality before the law
destroyed by inequality before the judge, in short, the lie
in the programme of '89 which replaced great names by
big coins and turned marquises into bankers—nothing
more than that. Yet it was a novelist who saw through
all that."

CHAPTER VIII

DEATH OF THE HERO

IT seems an unnecessary platitude to emphasize that a novel should be chiefly concerned with the creation of character. Unfortunately, except in a formal sense, this is no longer in fact the chief concern of modern novelists. Novels to-day are concerned with almost everything but. human character. Some, like those of Mr. Huxley, are concerned with the *Encyclopædia Britannica* and the idiosyncrasies of one's personal acquaintances, others, like those of D. H. Lawrence, are highly coloured descriptions of the author's own moods, or else they are political arguments, like the majority of the works of H. G. Wells, or mild social satire, like a hundred books by Tom, Jane, Emily and Harry (certainly, social satire is a legitimate theme for the novelist, has indeed produced some of the world's greatest novels, but even the satirist, or rather, the satirist above all, is not exempt from the obligation to make human character the centre of his work).

Human personality, however, has disappeared from the contemporary novel, and with it the "hero." The process of killing off the hero was inevitable in the development of the nineteenth-century novel. The decay of realism compelled it. Flaubert, in writing *Madame Bovary,* was still chiefly interested in the woman herself, though his creative method made him expend his energy almost as much on the painting of a perfect genre picture of the Norman province as on the personality of Emma. But Edmond de Goncourt was already thinking in terms of writing a novel about the stage, about a hospital, about prostitution, rather than about people. Zola continued with novels on war, on money, on prostitution, on the Paris

markets, on alcoholism, and so on. Arnold Bennett, the
faithful disciple of the French realists, wrote an excellent
novel about his father and his own youth, and then,
seized with the fatal desire to write "the history of a
family" ruined his early work by two sequels. Similarly,
he wrote one of the best novels of pre-war England about
two old ladies whom he had known in the Potteries, and
then descended to writing about a newspaper proprietor,
an hotel, prostitution (yes, indeed, just like a hundred
others!) and so on.

The Goncourts were careful artists, and it is still possible
to read their works with some pleasure. Zola had all the
vitality and creative power of genius and his novels are
also still readable because of the passion in them. But all
the thousands of "realist" studies by those who are neither
artists nor men of passion and genius are unreadable
within a month of publication day. The modern novelist,
abandoning the creation of personality, of a hero, for the
minor task of rendering ordinary people in ordinary
circumstances, has thereby abandoned both realism and
life itself. This is true not only of the professed realists of
the "objective" school, but also of the novelists of purely
subjective psychological analysis. Indeed, the latter can
claim the credit for having reduced the creation of
character to absurdity, even though to an occasionally
magnificent and talented absurdity, for James Joyce is so
determined to portray the ordinary man that he takes
the most ordinary, "mean" man he can find in Dublin,
and so intent is he on picturing him in "ordinary" cir-
cumstances that he introduces his hero perched on the
closet seat.

This is in effect the denial of humanism, of the whole
Western tradition in literature (indeed, of the common
view of man that world literature as a whole gives us, for
the East has its humanism also). The whole modern
approach to the problem of creation is by means of the

isolation of life from reality, and eventually, through the destruction of time and the inner logic of events, the mutual interaction of the characters and the outer world is lost; it is an approach which in the end kills creation by denying the historical character of man. Indeed, the bourgeoisie cannot any longer accept man in time, man acting in the world, man changed by the world and man changing the world, man actively creating himself— historical man, because such acceptance implies condemnation of the bourgeois world, recognition of the historical fate of capitalism and of the forces at work in society which are changing it.

In the novels of the great period of the nineteeth century the hero whom we meet most frequently is the young man in conflict with society and finally disillusioned or vanquished by it. He is Stendhal's only hero, Balzac frequently puts him in the centre of the stage, he is the principle figure of almost every Russian novel, and you can find him in England also from Pendennis down to Richard Feverel, Ernest Pontifex and Jude. This irreconcilable youth, idealistic, passionate and unhappy, is the individualist who cannot fit in to the society which accepts egoism for a religion. For it seems that the century recognized two forms of egoism, sacred and profane, and for the sacred egoists there was no place, only despair, hypocrisy, the breaking of the will and eventual loss of faith.

This youthful hero, it is safe to assume, was in most cases only the imaginative re-creation of the author's own youth, or of some phase of his personal struggle with a society that did not and could not accept his humanism, his views on personal happiness, on property, on the relations between the sexes. Flaubert's letters are full of his bitter hatred and contempt for the bourgeois society which would compel the artist to conform at every point to its petty ideals of respectability founded in ignorance and supported on a solid basis of hard cash. Flaubert and his fellow-intellectuals, among them many of the best and most honest minds of the nineteenth century, saw the root of all social evil in compulsory education and universal suffrage. For them the first meant education in conformity to bourgeois ideals and the second was identified in their minds with the plebiscite which had confirmed in power the bourgeois dictatorship of Napoleon the Little.

The reaction against the monotony, the baseness of life in capitalist society of the nineteenth century prevented the novelist from understanding and mastering some of the most interesting aspects of human life in the century. That he should, on the whole, have ignored the working class was natural. The novelist had no ·contact with the worker, looked upon him as the inhabitant of a strange, incomprehensible world, and only later, after the Paris Commune, began seriously the difficult effort of exploring that world. Edmond de Goncourt writes frankly that he feels like a police spy when gathering the materials for a novel of "low life," but that he is drawn to it "perhaps because I am a well-born literary man, and the people, the 'canaille,' if you like, attract me like an unknown, undiscovered nation, with something of the 'exotic' that travellers look for with a thousand sufferings in distant lands." For most writers the working class have still merely this attraction of the "exotic," regardless of the fact that it is impossible to create human personality from such a viewpoint. With one or two rare exceptions (Mark Rutherford, for example) the novelist has never succeeded in drawing convincing men and women of the working class, and, because of this difficulty in breaking down the barrier between "the two nations," has rarely even tried the task.

But it is more remarkable that two other types of man should have been excluded from imaginative literature by the bourgeois novelist, two types who really played a decisive part in the history of capitalist society, the scientist and the capitalist "leader," the millionaire ruler of our modern life.

Of the world's supreme scientists, Archimedes, Galileo, Newton, Lavoisier, Darwin, Faraday, Pasteur and Clerk Maxwell, four are Englishmen and three of these are Englishmen of the nineteenth century. Humphry Davy, first of the great physical scientists in nineteenth century England, was the intimate friend of Southey, Coleridge, Wordsworth and the novelist Maria Edgeworth. There can have been few more interesting Englishmen than the chemist Dr. Joseph Priestley, yet he has not even had the tribute of a good biography (possibly because he was neither a Jesuit, an eccentric, nor a Tory). You may search in vain through the work of the really good novelists of the nineteenth century for so much as a recognition that the existence of science should mean more to man than the existence of public lavatories, a useful, necessary, but unpleasant convenience. Both are excluded from the field of literature. Even in our own day, when science is fully recognized and the lavatory has its honoured place in literature, it is only a few rather second-hand writers who have recognized the right of the scientist to be placed at least on a par with the prostitute and the actress as a subject for art.

Do not imagine that this is a plea for the scientist to be recognized as "a subject" as de Goncourt recognized the actress or Zola the slaughter-house and Arnold Bennett the luxury hotel. The scientist is not a subject, he is a type of man whose creative mind approaches that of the great artist, he is a part of human life and no possible picture of human life in the modern world is complete which ignores him. There are two reasons why this kind of man, one of the really creative forces of our time, has been ignored by the novelist. The first is that the novelist is himself so ignorant of science, so apart and separated from the region of scientific creation in this world of narrow specialization and division of labour, that the whole of this vital field of the human personality remains a closed book for him. The second reason is that the very conditions of social life have prevented the novelist from exploring the scientific personality. Science is one of the demiurges of our world, yet it is also enslaved and corrupted by our world. It would have demanded a fearless realist to portray the scientist in the nineteenth century, one who would have been willing to brave religion and the prejudices of the ignorant, as well as to expose commercial corruption and the roots of the social system. And in our own day he would have to be ready to go even further, to show society using science to destroy science.

I have mentioned that the novelist ignored one other development of human personality, not the least important in the century, by any means. In all the considerable achievement of the nineteenth and twentieth centuries in fiction you will search in vain for a picture of the great business man, the man who organized the building of railways, the construction of steel mills, the getting of diamonds out of the African earth, and the cutting of canals through the swamps and deserts to link up the oceans. Perhaps the nineteenth century novelists are not so much to blame here. Before 1870 the man who really counted in business was the banker and Balzac dealt faithfully with him. The manufacturer was a relatively small man who had not yet allied himself with finance to rule the world, and, in fact, this small manufacturer or business man is not ignored by the great realists. It is otherwise in the last third of the century and in our own day. Where is Cecil Rhodes, or Rockefeller, or Krupp? Dreiser alone has tried to picture the career of such a man, but in general the artist has shied away from him as from the devil. Yet there is no reason why the devil should be denied imaginative treatment. Milton found him quite amenable. And if Edward Campion, the Jesuit Martyr, is worthy of the attention of a talented writer, then why not Ivar Kreuger, capitalist martyr to the collapse of the god "prosperity"?

The artist of the Renaissance did not shrink from describing a villain. Shakespeare would have said that life was not complete without a villain. It would be very unfair to imagine that the villain is merely negative, that he has no positive features or is a mere symbolic embodiment of evil. True, your modern capitalists only superficially resemble the Renaissance adventurers. Where the latter were violent, bloody and cruel in the open, the former are so in the dark, or leave the violence and cruelty entirely to their agents; where the Renaissance prince was grandly lecherous in a wild experimental way, as though he were discovering life in the human body, your modern plutocrat is inclined to secret perversions, and his orgies resemble more a Folies Bergères revue than a Borgia's banquet.

Yet there are remarkable men among the plutocrats. Rhodes was as remarkable as he was unpleasant. Northcliffe was a genius as well as a madman. You cannot separate these men from much of the poetry of modern life, from the conquest of matter that made possible the modern newspaper which can give you a photograph of a king dying from an assassin's bullet almost as soon as the shot is fired, thanks to the discoveries of modern physics. The movements of great nations, the passionate sacrifices of men and women for mighty causes, are also bound up with the lives of plutocrats.

They have no place, however, in imaginative literature, the writer shrinks from them, fears the awful forces that will be let loose in his pages if once he tries to re-create such a personality in fiction. Better therefore to take the quiet world of Swann, the gardens, the drawing-rooms, the long conversations and the delicate analyses of feeling, the more refined perversions of flesh and spirit; these are, it is true, the reflections of the world of your millionaires who own the lives of nations and control the fate of great civilizations, but they are reflections so delicately isolated, so far removed from the real world that created Swann, the Duchess and Monsieur de Charlus, that we may safely ignore this world's existence.

So in our modern novel both hero and villain have died. Personality no longer exists except in iridescent cuttings pasted on the microscope slide. Such cuttings are often exceedingly curious, interesting or beautiful, but they are not living men and women. With the destruction of personality, replaced by the average individual in the average situation, or by an aspect of a personality mechanically isolated in a part of his consciousness, has gone the destruction of the novel's structure, its epic character. Man is no longer the individual will in conflict with other wills and personalities, for to-day all conflict must be overshadowed by the immense social conflicts shaking and transforming modern life, and so conflict also disappears from the novel, being replaced by subjective struggles, sexual intrigues, or abstract discussion.

In place of a unified philosophical outlook that was maintained with some success (despite the divergent trends of materialism and idealism) from the Renaissance to Kant, from the sixteenth to the end of the eighteenth century, there has come a complete collapse of any unified world outlook, a philosophical electicism, the decadent pseudo-philosophies of will and intuition of Nietzsche and Bergson, the erotic mysticism of Freud, the subjective idealism of the various neo-Kantian schools, and finally the denial of the human reason, the renunciation of the Renaissance and of humanism, which are the inevitable outcome of this philosophical decadence, itself only a reflection of the desperate agonies of political counterrevolution. Our civilization began with Erasmus, Rabelais and Montaigne. It ends with the return to mediaevalism, the doctrines of blood and race, with religious and erotic mysticism, Spengler, Otman Spann, Freud and the rest. The grand first declaration of independence of the individual becomes in our time no more than a declaration of the death of the individual in the name of the sanctity of individualism.

In the absence of a world outlook, of an understanding of life, no full and free expression of human personality is possible. The novel cannot find new life, humanism cannot be reborn, until such an outlook has been attained. That outlook to-day can only be the outlook of dialectical materialism, giving birth in art to a new Socialist realism. Marx and Engels in their book *The Holy Family*, written as long ago as 1844, pointed out that humanism to-day has no meaning apart from Socialism. "If man constructs all his knowledge, perception, etc., from the world of sense and his experiences in the world of sense, then it follows that it is a question of so arranging the empirical world that he experiences the truly human in it, that he becomes accustomed to experiencing himself as a human being. . . . French and English socialism and Communism represented this coincidence of humanism and materialism in the realm of practice."

More than one reader will no doubt have objected as he read this argument that the generalizations are altogether too sweeping. Do we really have no creative writing (in this highest sense of imaginative creation of human character) in *Ulysses* or *Swann's Way*? Did not Wells in his early work, for all his own modest denials, succeed in giving us character, and Lawrence, and has not Huxley?

It is true that in the character of Bloom we do get from Joyce a human personality. But Bloom is the only character in Ulysses. Daedalus has not much more flesh and blood to him than Conrad's Marlowe, the various Dubliners encountered in that Odyssey of a day are simply reminiscences from the author's circle of acquaintance, good description, shrewd analysis, but not created characters. And Bloom himself, is this really a picture of a man? Perhaps it is 90 per cent of a man, photographed rather than created, yet it is most certainly not what the author would have us believe it to be, man abstracted and made into a symbol of all the "plain men" of the twentieth century. Bouvard and Pécuchet were also intended as a realistic photograph of the French Blooms, and they very nearly succeed in being something more, in becoming almost a heroic re-creation of the "little man" about whom we hear so much to-day. Yet not quite. Flaubert did not know anything about the modern psychological discovery of man's subconscious. Joyce did, and one cannot help thinking that it has not been altogether to his advantage. Flaubert, after all, though he was deprived by time of the new revelation of Freud, had at least read, enjoyed and understood Rabelais. Joyce had only hated the Jesuits.

Nor, I think, can Proust claim a much greater success than Joyce. True, he understands men and women better, but these world-weary ghosts in the Paris drawing-room are still only shadows. Some critics have suggested that Proust is not a novelist at all, but an essayist, a modern Montaigne. There is some truth in this, if we overlook the comparison with Montaigne. Proust cannot claim a place among the master novelists because he lacks the most important qualification, he has not mastered life with sufficient intensity to make his people live a complete life of their own, a life in which you can ask them any question and force an answer.

With Wells, Lawrence and Huxley, we are on a lower level. Kipps, Mr. Polly and the rest are little more than idealized projections of their own creator and such pathos as they have is his rather than their own. Huxley, I feel, has much in common with Wells, the same passion for ideas which gives a vitality to his books that they would never derive from their characters alone, the same interest in science and the same inability to come to any satisfactory conclusion with the hard facts of life in the contemporary world. He is, indeed, what Wells would have been if he had gone to Eton and Oxford instead of to Bromley Grammar School and South Kensington.

Lawrence has little claim to be considered a novelist at all, for after the brilliant beginning of *Sons and Lovers* and *The Rainbow*, he abandoned novel writing altogether for those strange, beautiful and mystical poems in prose which are the bulk of his stories and tales. Here are no men and women of flesh and blood, but simply moods. Compare, for example, *The Rainbow* with its deplorable sequel *Women in Love*. Who would ever believe that the abstractions of the latter novel had any relation at all to the passionate sisters in the first book? And how pale, how lifeless, is even that early theme of love and marriage in *The Rainbow* compared with Tolstoi's treatment of the same subject in the marriage of Levin and Kitty! Something happened to Lawrence after writing *The Rainbow* which completely destroyed his creative ability. His significance for the modern novelist, I think, lies not at all in his prophetic nonsense about the primitive, but in the fact that he was the last writer to appreciate English country and the beauty of the English earth. One cannot, however, think passionately even about English country and the English earth if one is unable to see that this earth is not free, that the heritage of every Englishman is being wantonly deformed and destroyed by a tiny group of ignorant and conscienceless landlords. Hardy had the ability to see this and Lawrence had not, so, though Lawrence wrote better English, it is Hardy's vision of the English country which is more compelling.

It is the central task of the English novelist to restore man to the place that belongs to him in the novel, to put in a complete picture of man, to understand and imaginatively re-create every phase of the personality of contemporary man. Man's consciousness is extended, it is bursting free of the bonds imposed on it by capitalist society, it is desirous of using all the wonderful opportunities modern life puts at its disposal through the growth of rapid communication by land and air, through the development of cinema, wireless and television, through the possibility of living in houses whence vile and degrading labour has been abolished. It cannot yet do these things. Only a very few men, the masters of the capitalist world, can use the wonderful creations of modern life, and these men use them, not for further development of the human spirit, but for its total destruction. Yet in almost every man and woman, in the Indian and Chinese as much as the Englishman and Frenchman, the consciousness that the enjoyment of life can even now be deepened and extended is there. That consciousness is being transformed into action, into the effort to make a new world. A new era of human liberation is beginning.

The question then arises, what manner of men and women are we to describe in our books? How are we to see human beings in action? To whom can we look for guidance? The new realism it is our task to create must take up the task where bourgeois realism laid it down. It must show man not merely critical, or man at hopeless war with a society he cannot fit into as an individual, but man in action to change his conditions, to master life, man in harmony with the course of history and able to become the lord of his own destiny. This means that the heroic must come back to the novel, and with the heroic its epic character. Hazlitt, writing of Shakespeare's characters compares them with Chaucer's, and gives us, in the course of the comparison, a clear understanding of

how a novelist who has a realist view of life should picture
men:

"Chaucer's characters are sufficiently distinct from one
another, but they are too little varied in themselves, too
much like identical propositions. They are consistent, but
uniform; we get no idea of them from first to last; they
are not placed in different lights, nor are their subordinate
traits brought out in new situations; they are like portraits
or physiognomical studies, with the distinguishing features
marked with inconceivable truth and precision, but that
preserve the same unaltered air and attitude. Shake-
speare's are historical figures, equally true and correct,
but put into action, where every nerve and muscle is
displayed in the struggle with others, with all the effect
of collision and contrast, with every variety of light and
shade. Chaucer's characters are narrative, Shakespeare's
dramatic, Milton's epic. That is, Chaucer told only as
much of his story as he pleased, as was required for a
particular purpose. He answered for his characters him-
self. In Shakespeare they are introduced upon the stage,
are liable to be asked all sorts of questions, and are forced
to answer for themselves. In Chaucer we perceive a fixed
essence of character. In Shakespeare there is a continual
composition and decomposition of its elements, a fermen-
tation of every particle in the whole mass, by its alternate
affinity or antipathy to other principles which are brought
into contact with it. Till the experiment is tried we do
not know the result, the turn which the character will
take in its new circumstances."

This view of character, entirely lost from the novel, is
the one that the revolutionary novelist must restore. Not
for him the fear of reality, the shrinking from showing
the full man. His is the task from which the novelists of
the bourgeoisie have turned away, to create, by his
imaginative effort, the typical man, the hero of our times,
and in this way to become, as Stalin has phrased it, "an
engineer of the human soul."

CHAPTER IX

SOCIALIST REALISM

FIELDING, in discussing the theory of the novel, always emphasized its epic and historical character. You cannot, he insists, show man complete unless you show him in action. The novelist, he writes in one of the introductory chapters to *Tom Jones*, is not a mere chronicler, but a historian. His work, therefore, should not resemble "a newspaper which consists of just the same number of words, whether there be any news in it or not." The novelist, as opposed to the chronicler, must use the method "of those writers, who profess to disclose the revolutions of countries." That is to say, he must be concerned with change, with the relation of cause and effect, with crisis and conflict, and not merely with description or subjective analysis.

He explains, in another chapter, even more exactly, the role of the novelist, who must possess the faculty of "penetrating into all things within our reach and knowledge, and of distinguishing their essential differences." The qualities here called for, he terms "invention and judgment," and at once denies that invention is simply the ability to create incident or a situation. "By invention is really meant no more (and so the word signifies) than discovery, or finding out; or to explain it at large, a quick and sagacious penetration into the true essence of all the objects of our contemplation. This, I think, can rarely exist without the concomitancy of judgment; for how we can be said to have discovered the true essence of two things, without discerning their difference, seems to me hard to conceive."

This is excellent sense, as excellent sense as any man

has ever written upon the writing of novels, and its author not unjustly heads the chapter of *Tom Jones* in which it is contained, "of those who lawfully may, and of those who may not, write such histories as this." The other qualities of a lawful novelist, or historian, as Fielding calls him, should be learning, and he mentions that Homer and Milton, the epic poets whom he acknowledges as his masters, "were masters of all the learning of their times," and after learning, the ability to "be universal with all ranks and degrees of men."

When the novelist again accepts Fielding's view of his functions, we shall have a new realism. Yes, a new realism, for clearly the discovery of the essence of things in our day, the ability to see essential differences, the ability to be universal with all men, cannot result in the mere restoration of the novel of Fielding or of Dickens. To-day penetration into the essential differences must mean the revelation of those contradictions which are the motive forces of human actions, both the inner contradictions in a man's character and those external contradictions with which they are inextricably connected. We cannot to-day be universal with all men unless we are able to understand how the relations between men have changed since Fielding's time.

Modern psychology has without doubt accumulated a mass of important material upon human character, in particular upon the deeper, subconscious elements in man, which the novelist must take into account. Yet this does not imply for a moment that these collections of psychological data can of themselves explain all human actions or human thoughts and emotions. Not all the work of Freud, Havelock Ellis or of Pavlov can allow the novelist to abdicate his function to the psychologist. The Marxist certainly denies the right of the psychologist to explain all processes of human thought or changes in the human psyche by purely subjective causes such as the Oedipus

complex or any other of the formidable array of complexes
in the psycho-analytical armoury. You cannot give a
picture of man in his individual "revolutions," as de-
manded by Fielding, you cannot truly penetrate the
human personality in order to re-create it imaginatively,
when bound by the purely biological view of the mental
life which is presented by Freud, or by the purely
mechanistic view of Pavlov and the reflexologists. Cer-
tainly, the modern psychologists have added enormously
to the store of our knowledge of man, and the novelist
who to-day neglected their contributions would be as
ignorant as he is foolish, but they have failed entirely to
see the individual as a whole, as a social individual.
They have provided the basis for that false outlook on
life which in Proust and Joyce has led to the sole aim of
art being, instead of the creation of human personality,
the dissociation of human personality.

Psycho-analysis, for all its brilliant and courageous
probing into the secret depths of the personality, has
never understood that the individual is only a part of
the social whole, and that the laws of this whole, decom-
posed and refracted in the apparatus of the individual
psyche like rays of light passing through a prism, change
and control the nature of each individual. Man to-day is
compelled to fight against the objective, external horrors
accompanying the collapse of our social system, against
Fascism, against war, unemployment, the decay of agri-
culture, against the domination of the machine, but he
has to fight also against the subjective reflection of all
these things in his own mind. He must fight to change
the world, to rescue civilization, and he must fight
also against the anarchy of capitalism in the human
spirit.

It is in this dual struggle, each side of which in turn
influences and is influenced by the other, that the end of
the old and artificial division between subjective and

objective realism will come. We shall no longer have the old naturalistic realism, no longer have the novel of endless analysis and intuition, but a new realism in which the two find their proper relationship to one another. Certainly, the modern realists, the heirs of Zola and of Maupassant, have felt the inadequacy of the method of their masters. But lack of dialectic, of a philosophy which enables them really to understand and to perceive the world, has led them along the false trail of supplementing that naturalism by a creaking, artificial symbolism. This is the gravest fault of those endless, powerful, but unsatisfactory works of Jules Romains and Céline.

How is it possible to make this combination, to break down the old division within bourgeois realism? First of all by restoring the historical view which was the basis of the classical English novel. Here let me emphasize that this does not imply merely the need for plot and narrative, for it is living man with whom we are concerned, and not merely the external circumstances in which man has his being. This is the mistake made by many Socialist novelists who have used all their talent and energy to depict a strike, a social movement, the construction of Socialism, a revolution or a civil war, without considering that what is supremely important is not the social background, but man himself in his full development against that background. Epic man is man in whom no division any longer occurs between himself and his sphere of practical activity. He lives and changes life. Man creates himself.

It is only the fairest self-criticism to acknowledge that neither the Soviet novel nor the novels of Western revolutionary writers have yet succeeded in fully expressing this, with a few rare exceptions. There is the best of excuses. The events themselves, the Russian civil war, the construction of socialist industry, the revolution in the life of the peasant, the fight against exploitation and the defence of the working class against Fascism, all these things appear so heroic, so impressive, that the writer feels that by merely writing them down the effect must be overwhelming. Indeed, it is often of the greatest emotional significance, but an emotional significance which, nevertheless, is only that of first-class journalism. The writers do not add thereby to our knowledge of man, or really extend our consciousness and sensibility.

The historical event, Engels wrote in the letter from which I quoted in the second chapter of this essay, is anything but a simple addition of $1 + 1 = 2$, a direct relation of cause and effect. "History makes itself in such a way that the final result always arises from conflicts between many individual wills, of which each again has been made what it is by a host of particular conditions of life. Thus there are innumerable intersecting forces, an infinite series of parallelograms of forces which give rise to one resultant—the historical event."

Both Engels and Marx considered Shakespeare to be the one author who solved in a supreme way the problem of the presentation of the human personality. Shakespeare's characters are their ideal of how the Marxist writer should present man, as being at one and the same time a type and an individual, a representative of the mass and a single personality. Engels in his interesting letters to Lassalle criticizing the latter's historical drama *Franz von Eickingen*, considers that the chief defect is Lassalle's adoption of Schiller's dramatic method in preference to Shakespeare's "realism." "You are perfectly right," Engels says, "to reject the prevalent stupid individualization, which comes down to mere petty philosophizing and represents an essential sign of a declining, epigone's literature. I think, though, that a personality is characterized not merely by what he does, but also by how he does it, and from that aspect it would not, I think, hurt the ideal content of your drama if the various characters were rather more sharply demarcated and opposed to one another. In our times the characterization of the *ancients* is already insufficient, and here, I think, you might well consider rather more the importance of Shakespeare in the history of the development of the drama."

Marx and Engels would certainly have agreed with Hazlitt's view of the Shakespearian treatment of character as "a continual composition and decomposition of its elements, a fermentation of every particle in the whole mass, by its alternate affinity or antipathy to other principles which are brought in contact with it. Till the experiment is tried, we do not know the result, the turn which the character will take in its new circumstances." This quality of unexpectedness, which shall at the same time be in accord with the inner logic of the historical event and of the character himself, is precisely what Engels had in mind when he wrote that what emerges from the conflict of individual wills "is something that no one willed."

It will be easily understood from what I have said so far of the Marxian view of realism that it does not at all correspond with the popular illusion concerning revolutionary, or proletarian, literature, that such literature is little more than a scarcely disguised political tract. Marx and Engels were clearly of the opinion that no author could write oblivious to the class struggles of his time, that all writers, consciously or unconsciously, take up a position on these struggles and express it in their work. Particularly is this so in the great creative periods of world literature. But for that form of writing which substitutes the opinions of the author for the living actions of human beings, they always possessed the greatest contempt. As early as 1851, in an article in the *New York Tribune*, Engels writes extremely critically of the literary movement in Germany from 1830 to 1848. "A crude Constitutionalism, or a still cruder Republicanism, were preached by almost all writers of the time. It became more and more the habit, particularly of the inferior sorts of literati, to make up for the want of cleverness in their productions, by political allusions which were sure to attract attention. Poetry, novels, reviews, the drama, every literary production teemed with what was called "tendency," that is, with more or less timid exhibitions of an anti-governmental spirit."

In the letter to Miss Harkness on Balzac, written nearly forty years later, he is even more explicit. "I am far from finding fault," he tells her, "with your not having written a pinchbeck Socialist novel, a *tendenz Roman* as we Germans call it, to glorify the social and political views of the author. That is not at all what I mean. The more the opinions of the author remain hidden, the better for the work of art. The realism I allude to, may crop out even in spite of the author's opinions." What Marx and Engels did insist upon, however, was that a work of art should conform to its author's outlook on the world, since only that outlook could give it artistic unity. But the author's own views must never obtrude. The outlook must not be preached, it should appear quite naturally from the circumstances and the characters themselves. This is true tendentiousness, the kind that has informed all great works of art, that can be seen, as Engels told yet another would-be Socialist novelist, Minna Kautsky, Karl's mother, in both Aeschylus and Aristophanes, in Dante and Cervantes, in the contemporary Russian and Norwegian novelists who "have produced splendid novels, all tendentious. But I think that tendency should arise of itself out of the situation and action, without being specially emphasized, and that an author is not obliged to give the reader a ready-made historical future solution of the social conflicts he depicts."

He develops this view further in the same letter by pointing out that in modern conditions the author's public must largely be drawn from the bourgeoisie, and that "therefore, in my view the Socialist tendentious novel completely fulfils its mission in describing real social relationships, in destroying relative illusions concerning them, in upsetting the optimism of the bourgeois world, in sowing doubt as to the eternal nature of the existing social order, even though the author did not thereby advance any definite solution and sometimes did not even come down on one side or the other."

It is not the author's business to preach, but to give a real, historical picture of life. It is only too easy to substitute lay figures for men and women, sets of opinions for flesh and blood, "heroes" and "villains" in the abstract for real people tortured by doubts, old allegiances, traditions and loyalties, but to do this is not to write a novel. Speeches mean nothing if one cannot understand all the processes of life behind any speech. Certainly characters may have, and should have, political opinions, provided they are their own and not the author's. Even though in some cases a character's opinions coincide with those of the author, they should be expressed with the voice of the character, and this in turn implies that the character must possess his own individual voice, his personal history.

A revolutionary writer is a party writer, his outlook is that of the class which is struggling to create a new social order, all the more reason therefore to demand from him the widest sweep of imagination, the utmost creative power. He fulfils his party mission by his work in creating a new literature, free from the anarchist individualism of the bourgeoisie in its period of decay, and not by substituting the slogans of the party on this or that question of the day for the real picture of the world his outlook demands from him. He will be unable to make that picture a true one unless he is truly a Marxist, a dialectician with a finished philosophical outlook. Or, as Fielding would have put it, unless he has made a real effort to master the learning of his time.

Such a view of the artist implies that he excludes nothing from his perception of life. Proletarian literature is still very young, less than ten years old outside of the Soviet Union, and the reproach has often been made that, at least in capitalist countries, it has tended to deal only with certain men and with limited aspects of these men. The strike-leader, the capitalist "boss," the intellectual seeking a new faith, beyond these, it is suggested, the new writers have not ventured far, and they have succeeded only to a slight extent in showing us even these characters as men of flesh and blood. The reproach is to some extent justified, though it ignores the epic stories of Malraux, the two novels of Ralph Bates, the work of John Dos Passos and Erskine Caldwell. Yet there is no human character, no emotion, no conflict of personalities outside the scope of the revolutionary novelist. Indeed, he alone is able to create the hero of our times, the complete picture of modern life, because only he is able to perceive the truth of that life. Yes, there have been few novels by revolutionaries free of those faults criticized by Marx and Engels. Much has yet to be done before the new literature is able to fulfil its tasks, and it will always remain true that you must have great novelists before you get great novels. On the other hand, the sceptic would do well to remember that in the grim battle of ideas in the world of to-day, the majority of the best of the writers of the bourgeoisie have begun to move sharply to the Left and that this movement has brought them into contact with declaredly revolutionary writers. From this contact we may be justified in hoping there will come the fertilization of genius which we are seeking, for it should have been made sufficiently clear in this essay that the revolutionary both accepts all that is vital and hopeful in the heritage of the past, and rejects nothing in the present which can be used to build the future.

CHAPTER X

MAN ALIVE

WHAT sort of man are you going to show in your new picture of life? the reader may feel inclined to ask at this point. How are you going to get that stubborn, wayward, quarrelsome and passionate creature into the pages of your book? Man at war within and without himself, man suffering, man in love, man hating, man defending his property, revolutionary man, what are you going to do about him?

Fair questions, though difficult to answer. Let us try one of these men, the revolutionary, and, in particular, the revolutionary of the working class. After all, though not every revolutionary novel is bound to portray revolutionaries, or even the life of the working class, such novels must in the end stand or fall by their ability to create an artistic picture of the revolutionary as a type and as an individual man. So far, let us admit it, we have not succeeded. The least credible figures in the novels written about revolution are the revolutionaries. This is true even of the very best of these novels, by men like Sholokhov, Malraux or Bates. Sholokhov's Communist heroes have energy, force, will-power, they are alive and they are convincing, but they are nevertheless flat surfaces, rather than men in the round. Malraux and Bates draw characters who are rarely convincing as men but often as Communists. The psychology of the professional revolutionary (the man whose whole life is devoted to revolutionary organization and leadership) is not that of the Malraux or the Bates hero.

Of course, we must remember that the revolutionary in the sense of the individual whose life is devoted to the service of a revolutionary cause, is a new character created by capitalist society, particularly in the nineteenth century. He appears in the work of Victor Hugo; Flaubert acknowledges his existence, but only sees him in his worst form, the lower middle-class politician of 1848, the type analysed with such deadly truth in the works of Marx and Engels on the revolution of '48; Meredith also, strangely enough, is attracted by him and tries to give a picture of the Italian revolutionary nationalist in *Vittoria* and *Sandro Bellini*.

Dostoievsky and Turgeniev, attracted and repelled at the same time by the Russian anarchist movement, take the strange, revolting figure of Nechaiev, Bakunin's friend and evil genius, and using his image they try, unjustly, to pillory the whole of the Russian progressive movement of the mid-century in their novels *The Possessed* and *Smoke*. Much later, in our own time, Conrad used Nechaiev for the same purpose in his novel *Under Western Eyes*, though Conrad had a different political aim from his greater predecessors.

One thing distinguishes all these novelists. They took their revolutionaries from the petty-bourgeoisie, from the nationalist, democratic or anarchist movements of the last century. They build up his image critically, now repelled by this individualist in political revolt against society, now attracted by certain features in him. When we think of them, we have to admit that Marx and Engels, revolutionaries themselves, made a much more severe, yet much more satisfactory attack on this type of revolutionary, more satisfactory because they saw his relation to the real revolutionary of our day, the revolutionary of the working class against capitalist society. Their criticism was not negative, it was the active criticism of two men seeking to arm humanity for the greatest task in its history.

The working-class revolutionary nevertheless did make his appearance in nineteenth-century literature, and not unworthily. Zachariah Coleman, Mark Rutherford's printer hero of the *Revolution in Tanner's Lane*, has the vitality that makes immortality. The novel itself has glaring faults, almost all possible faults, in fact, but it lives by the sincere and powerful force of its characterization, Zachariah, Jean Caillaud, the two Paulines, by the sober prose which expresses so perfectly those passionate and unhappy democrats.

Zachariah "was by nature a poet; essentially so, for he loved everything which lifted him above what is commonplace. Isaiah, Milton, a storm, a revolution, a great passion—with these he was at home." There is no gap in his life between the poetry of his vision and the prose of his life. The poverty, the first unhappy marriage, the bitterness of oppression, the prison, the religious doubt, all these in Zachariah become his indomitable will to change life, his poetry of revolution which finds for a moment its earthly satisfaction in his second marriage with Pauline.

This union of prose and poetry in his life keeps him loyal to himself so that at the end of his life the old republican can tell the radical ironmonger from Tanner's Lane: "I believe in insurrection . . . Insurrection strengthens the belief of men in the right. . . . Insurrection strengthens, too, the faith of others. When a company of poor men meet together and declare that things have got to such a pass that they will either kill their enemies or die themselves, the world then thinks there must, after all, be *some* difference between right and wrong."

Your revolutionary printer from Long Acre or Shoe Lane would express himself differently to-day, but he would not be what he is if Zachariah Coleman and thousands like him had not lived. Coleman's simplicity, his naïve belief that good must triumph over evil, are sometimes pathetic to us when we see them so easily abused, yet his force, his poetry, his belief in his class are still a source from which the revolutionary of to-day can draw his strength. In the course of the novel Coleman's faith never changes, but he himself does, he lives, he is beaten, he will not surrender, and his character develops in his battle with life.

Another and a greater book than Rutherford's is, however, the true revolutionary epic of the century. Certainly, it is a historical novel, its subject is the war of liberation of the Flemish people against their Spanish oppressors, and at times it is perhaps closer even to folklore than to history. Yet the author of *Tyl Ulenspiegel*, Charles de Coster, was well aware that his novel was a revolutionary one for our time also. In that Introduction which the late Sir Edmund Gosse spared the delicacy of English readers, de Coster is emphatic on the modern uses of his Owl Glass, and does not hesitate to say that there are other Spaniards and other Inquisitors to be fought and vanquished in our own day. Here again is the poetry of revolution merged with the prose of life, only the inspiration of de Coster's poetry was the folklore of Flanders, rather than that Old Testament which inspired Zachariah Coleman.

De Coster not only wrote a modern epic in the real sense, he showed an intuition, a psychological knowledge far beyond his time, such as none of our disciples of Freud has ever equalled. For a good reason, since his psychology was the result of the observation of life and not learned second-hand from text-books. In this book in which the poetry of earth and of common life, gross good humour, warm sensuality, faithful love, courage and devotion are mingled with hatred of the rich and powerful, loathing of humbug and hypocritical religion, is expressed the very essence of man's revolt against oppression. It is a world book. Tyl, when he bursts from his grave, sneezing and shaking the sand from his hair, is the symbol of the resurrection of the ordinary man to fight for a world where man has no dual values, but only himself, free and master of life. He scares the burgomaster and the alderman, those wretched representatives of the world of the Pharisees, and seizes by the throat the curé who had praised God for the death of Ulenspiegel the Beggar.

"'Inquisitor!' said Tyl, 'thou dost thrust me into the earth alive in my sleep. Where is Nele? hast thou buried her, too? Who art thou?'

The curé cried out:

'The great Beggar returneth into this world. Lord God! receive my soul!'

And he took to flight like a stag before the hounds.

Nele came to Ulenspiegel.

'Kiss me, my darling,' said he. . . . 'Can any bury,' said he, 'Ulenspiegel the spirit and Nele the heart of Mother Flanders? She, too, may sleep, but not die. No! Come, Nele.'

And he went forth with her, singing his sixth song, but no man knoweth where he sang the last one of all."

That last song is still to be sung, but we know the burden of it.

"And the will-o'-the-wisps said:

'The fire, 'tis we, vengeance for the bygone tears, the woes of the people; vengeance for the lords that hunted human game upon their lands; vengeance for the fruitless battles, the blood spilt in prisons, men burned and women and girls buried alive; vengeance for the fettered and bleeding past. The fire, 'tis we: we are the souls of the dead.'

At these words the Seven (vices) were changed to wooden statues, Ulenspiegel set fire to them so that they were burned and reduced to ashes, a river of blood ran down, and from out of the ashes rose up seven other shapes; the first said:

'Pride was I named; I am called Noble Spirit.' The

others spake in the same fashion, and Ulenspiegel and Nele saw from Avarice came forth Economy; from Anger, Vivacity; from Gluttony, Appetite; from Envy, Emulation, and from Idleness, the Reverie of poets and sages. And Lust upon her goat was transformed into a beautiful woman whose name was Love.

And the will-o'-the-wisps danced about them in a happy round.

Then Ulenspiegel and Nele heard a thousand voices of concealed men and women, sonorous and laughing voices that sang with a sound as of castanets:

> When over land and sea shall reign
> In form transfigured all these seven,
> Men, boldly raise your heads to Heaven;
> The Golden Age has come again."

These two books, *Revolution in Tanner's Lane* and *Ulenspiegel*, gain much of their force from being soaked in the national spirit, in the spirit of the people of England and of Belgium. Coleman is flesh and blood of all the struggles of the poor people of England, he comes straight from the Luddites, through the Puritans of the seventeenth century to the Wesleyan miners of the eighteenth and so to the early Chartists. He is a militant Protestant of the kind which has never been acceptable to our rulers, and his fierce protestantism is still continued to-day, stripped now of its religious covering, in the modern Labour movement. Tyl is Robin Hood and Coleman mixed, he is earth and spirit, the sturdy Beggar and the answer of man's soul to the Inquisition. He is folk-lore made life to stir our own blood until it runs warmer and quicker.

The contemporary writer finds no such ease in writing of the common man as did de Coster or "Mark Rutherford." The working man or woman torments him. It is not simply because working people **are** inarticulate.

Many of them are so, but as a whole they are not more noticeably inarticulate than the mass of human beings. A certain school of American writers, of which Hemingway is the best known, has created a type of brutal, but simple and inarticulate working man. He is hard-boiled, and the genius of Hemingway has made for him a forceful, simple speech of monosyllables with which he goes out uncomplainingly, because unconsciously, to meet his unenviable fate as boxer, bull-fighter, gun-man, quick-lunch server, stable-boy or soldier. "Dumb cattle" Wyndham Lewis has termed this working people of the American novelists. They certainly are very passive material for that malignant dirty deal which life so continually hands them.

Is this a true picture of the worker? It is certainly not. Even the London casual worker of the seventies and eighties, that most miserable of human beings, could hardly be said to fit this picture. Engels protested vigorously against the tendency, common to some Socialist novelists as well as to your modern American individualist, to picture the working class as a dumb and unresisting mass. He condemns this attitude in the letter to Miss Harkness from which I have quoted before:

"Realism, to my mind, implies, besides truth of detail, the true reproduction of typical characters in typical circumstances. Your characters are typical enough as far as they go; but the same cannot be said of the circumstances in which they move and which drive them to action. In *City Girl* (the title of Miss Harkness's novel), the working class figures as a passive mass, incapable of helping itself, not even desiring to make the effort to help itself. All attempts to get out of this deadening poverty proceed from outside, from above (in the words of Saint-Simon that class is 'la plus pauvre, la plus souffrante, la plus nombreuse,' 'the poorest, most debased class,' as Robert Owen says). But if this was a true description in

1800 or 1810, the time of Saint-Simon or Robert Owen, it is not so in 1887, especially for a man who for almost fifty years has had the honour of participating in the struggle of the militant proletariat and has always been guided by the principle that the emancipation of the working class must be at the act of the working class itself. The revolutionary resistance of the working class against the oppression of its environment, its feverish attempts, conscious or half-conscious, to obtain its human rights are a part of history and may demand a place in the sphere of realism."

This false view of the working class with which Engels reproaches Miss Harkness is held in our own day by the great majority of intellectuals and particularly of fiction writers. If anything, they hold it with even greater force, for they feel that on the one hand the growth of extreme mechanization, expressed in mass production, has destroyed the worker's personal initiative, converting him into a mere appendix of the machine; on the other hand, overcome by horror of Fascism, they are inclined to blame the worker, whose machine-like obedience, in their view, makes such mass slavery possible. In this way their complaints are an echo of Flaubert's, who blamed the masses for having helped create (through universal suffrage) the dictatorship of Louis Napoleon Bonaparte.

Nothing could be farther from the truth of working-class life. A mere glance at strike statistics and a summary of the causes of strikes, is enough to prove the falseness of such a conception. In fact, it is the working class alone which struggles against the effort to convert the mass of mankind into mechanical robots, the working class alone which bears the burden of the battle against the offensive of the machine or man. Not a day passes without some incident, of greater or less gravity, occurring in every factory of any size. It may be an isolated and trivial individual protest, such as swearing at a charge hand, or it may be a more serious collective action, but the battle is unceasing.

Plays by Elmer Rice and others of the "expressionist" school, Huxley's *Brave New World*, dozens of such books, plays and films have fostered the idea of the growth of a mechanical man, uniformed, a cipher, a mere working ant. It is a hopeless distortion of the truth, the consequence of the intellectual's isolation from the real human struggle of the age, of his despair at being unable to see any force at work against the mechanization he dreads. Yet every strike, indeed every day of life in the workshop, develops individual initiative, resource, courage and character as part of the revolt of man against this effort to enforce the enslavement of his body and mind, against the mechanical pressure of his environment. Certainly, one cannot overlook that the effort at enslavement in the factory is accompanied by an even more dangerous and tremendous offensive on men's minds. We rarely read a newspaper, watch a film, criticize a play or novel, objectively, from the standpoint of the established values of civilized life. If we were to use these values. as our criterion, it would be hard to resist the conclusion that most of the mass-produced intellectual life of our age was the product of raving madmen, suffering from every form of mental and moral perversion.

The educational system, firmly in the hands of capitalism, makes it more difficult for men and women to resist this insidious attack on their minds through the medium of the senses. Corruption, spiritual corruption, is widespread, and forms a terrible obstacle to the victorious issue of our common efforts against the ravages of this mental dry-rot. Yet even here, the working class is anything but passive, it struggles harder against this vilest form of corruption than do the despairing intellectuals. What else is the meaning of the thousands of self-education circles, the rambling clubs, the cinema and theatre societies, the Left Book Club with its great membership? If only the intellectuals were to join as wholeheartedly into this organization of resistance they would have less cause for complaint (some, to their honour, have joined in). The main difficulty is, the failure of the intellectual to understand clearly that the corruption which rightly appals him is not the consequence of a moral disease, but of a social system in decay. It is not the machine in itself, any more than the cinema in itself which is to blame, but the private ownership of machine and cinema alike.

This daily resistance to the horrors of the mass-production regime in the factory must, and does, eventually pass outside the factory. It becomes, in its highest form, resistance to war, to Fascism, to political reaction in every form, it becomes conscious defence of human culture, it brings about great heroic actions of the people and creates heroes, new types of men and women. Few would disagree with the view that in our time there is one example of moral grandeur and courage worthy to stand beside the greatest in our human history, the defence of Dimitrov against the Fascist court in Leipzig. Yet Dimitrov, the man, was forged in this very struggle which I have just described. The Bulgarian working-printer first grew mentally and morally in the work of organizing his fellow-workers into trade unions, then he led them, from 1912 to 1918, in the fight against war, then, in 1923, against Fascism which had lawlessly overthrown the democratic government of his country, and finally, in the Leipzig court, he appeared as the defender of all humanity and its culture against the advance of Fascist barbarism. Like Socrates, he could have claimed to have spent his whole life in preparing for his defence.

Indeed, this story of the Reichstag arson is an epic of our time which demands that the artist should give it life. The atmosphere is unforgettable: Berlin on the eve of Hitler's coup, a kind of feverish madness in the streets and beer-halls, those who should have been seeing to their weapons still repeating to themselves that no danger existed, those whose lives were at stake, understanding that democracy, in refusing unity, had betrayed the fortress to the enemy, busily preparing to continue the desperate fight in secret; and in the aristocratic clubs, the Ministries, the newspaper offices, the General Staff, constant intrigue, buying and selling of support, preparation for a war of extermination on the democracy of Germany.

In the midst of this the dull-witted, perverted pyromaniac, Van der Lubbe, is wandering in the outskirts of Berlin, sleeping in doss-houses, talking brave stuff to the scum he meets wearing the National-Socialist uniform, consumed with an idiot hatred of society, on that dangerous border-line of sanity that fitted in so well with the atmosphere of those days. He is probably mad already, though the police-spies, homosexual storm-troopers, local Nazi officials whom he meets are unable to see it. He goes out in the night to commit his petty little arsons, gloats over the flames so easily extinguished, and, inspired by the provocative frenzy of the Nazi press, sees himself hero of a great conflagration, burning down the corrupt Reichstag where all those talkers sell the poor man to his enemies. The Nazi spies pass on his ravings, by chance they get to the right quarters, and the stage is set, the flames are lit as the signal for that dreamed-of St. Bartholomew of the Nazi mythology.

Into this witch's Sabbath, accidentally there fall three sane men, Bulgarian communist refugees. They are seized, give Hitler the very chance he needs, three Balkan "barbarians" to answer for his fire and convince the world he is really saving civilization from a greater fire. Next, a typical German lower middle-class man, timid, level-headed, respectable, Torgler by name, is so shocked by the charge that he could have had anything to do with the crazy act of burning down the Reichstag in which he has played such an important part as leader of the Communist deputies, that he gives himself up to the police to prove its falseness by his own incontrovertible innocence. After all, the German courts may be a little prejudiced, the police a little brutal, but they are not mad, he reasons.

In prison the four men are chained day and night. Two of the Bulgarians understand no German, they are separated from one another, hear no news of the outer world, only understand they are threatened with a horrible, degrading death for something that seems so crazy as to be almost unbelievable. They are beaten, refused anything to read, kept for a time in semi-darkness as well as in chains. They don't fear death, having faced both death and torture in the prisons of their own country. But there at least you knew that outside were your own people, fighting your battle with you. Here they seem sunk in a black pit of madness, in which the headman's axe is the only sinister light to relieve the darkness. One of them, tormented by that vision, tells himself that if he must die, he will die cleanly, and opens a vein in his wrist. He does not die. They both refuse to surrender, but they do not fight, they see no way to struggle for that contact with the sane world of life which can alone support them.

Torgler is soon shown his mistake. The captors delight in degrading the self-respect of their "respectable" victim. They tell him he is to be shot, take him down a dark corridor, put a revolver at the back of his head so that he screams with fear. He is not any longer virtue defending his innocence, only a badly scared man, determined to try and keep some outward semblance of self-respect, but no more than that.

Dimitrov goes through all this. He is different, however, from the others. He sees the position as part of his whole life, and in that life he has never yet surrendered, never accepted a position of inferiority. He hits back from the beginning. His whole mind is concentrated on one thing only, how to turn the tables on the enemy. He knows they are prisoners whose lives are to be used as an excuse for a massacre, that if they fail to turn the tables, the madman's version of the fire will be accepted by the world and the cause of his class, which is that of humanity, will suffer a terrible set-back.

The other two Bulgarians knew no German, but they did not try to learn it. Dimitrov knew German quite well, and saw at once he must learn to know it even better in order to fight victoriously and so he studied, chains on his hands and feet, German grammars, the works of Goethe, German history, for he felt that this would also prove an excellent weapon. His mind was busy all day, all night, on how he could re-establish contact with the outer world, above all with his comrades in the Soviet Union. Failure followed failure, till at last he remembered the little spa in the hills of the North Caucasus, from which, in clear weather, the whole range of snow-clad mountains, dominated by Elbruz, is visible. He had rested there in the Sanatorium of the Central Committee. The doctor in charge was a Communist, there would be many active Party workers resting there as he had rested, taking the mineral water baths and climbing up through the Gardens to the windy Temple of Air facing the snowy, fortress-like Elbruz. A harmless little letter to this doctor living far away from Moscow, surely the Censors would pass it! They did. And so the campaign outside the prison grew, the forces began to rally, and the captives were alone no longer.

He read Shakespeare, to help his English, because he felt something in the poet, some mastery of life, that made his mind work quicker, strengthened the grip on life of his own will. He noted Hamlet's words: "To thine own self be true and it shall follow, as the night the day, thou canst not then be false to any man." Loyalty, loyalty to his own life, to his Communist convictions, was his dominating passion, his road to life. The thought of death did not often trouble him. He thought not so much of possible death as of the urgent need to win, to defeat his enemies, to turn his trial into a mighty condemnation of Fascism which should damage it irreparably. The atmosphere of madness never afflicted him, because he was himself so supremely sane that he knew he could not fail.

Do you want humour also in the story? There is plenty of it, even though a rather sinister, mad humour; the busy police officials, the Nazi leaders, building their crazy edifice of false testimony, dragging in silly land-ladies, burglars, maniacs of all kinds, all the festering respectability of the decaying middle class, all the strange borderland of crime and mental disease, to condemn these four men; the fantastic evidence of Goebbels and Goering, routed by the sharp wit and keen mind of the captive printer, the obsequious folly of the learned judge, here is enough material for a great comedian. Do you want the atmosphere of the mad-hatter's tea party, surely the witnesses in that trial will give it!

And all the time there is the figure of Van der Lubbe, the one man who could have told the truth, bowed, heavy, speechless, the very symbol of human degradation, of man with everything lost, emptied of his soul, the "wretched Faust" of this Mephistophelian drama.

The drama is too harsh, too masculine, objects the tender-hearted reader. Perhaps you want love? In prison Dimitrov hears of the death of his wife, the Serbian working girl, trade unionist, poetess, companion and fellow-fighter. We can guess a little of his feelings from a phrase in a letter to his mother; Lyuba, his wife, he writes, is also a heroine, "our unforgettable Lyuba."

There is that other love of a woman for him, his mother's, the old woman with the peasant's worn face, who has given all her children to the revolution and lost two of them. She thinks in Biblical phrases. Her son George is for her "the apostle Paul."

Of course, no modern novelist would handle such a subject if he were unable to find a suitable opportunity for a little amusing psychologizing. How then, about taking Dimitrov's landlady, who had those wonderful German betrothal cards printed to announce her non-existent engagement to her fascinating lodger? To this middle-class German woman, he was her unattainable ideal, her heavenly bridegroom.

I have said enough about the possibilities of the subject, and what, after all, you may fairly ask, has this long digression to do with the subject of my book? It may perhaps be excused as an attempt to show that in our modern life there are extraordinary subjects crying out for imaginative treatment, subjects in which the fantastic is mingled with the heroic, brutality with the calm spirit of man, baseness with loyalty and the chuckling of the insane with the searing wit of the mind's courage. Out of it all emerges a personality the study of which can only enlarge our experience and knowledge of man, strengthen our belief in our own powers and deepen our perception of life.

For do not believe that Dimitrov was born ready equipped for that battle of Leipzig. His life had been a long effort to overcome and re-mould himself as well as a battle against the semi-feudal capitalism of his Balkan country. Those of us who remember him after the defeat of the Bulgarian insurrection of 1923, know the moral fires he passed through in the following years. He spent a long time in fighting with himself, in merciless self-criticism. That failure showed he was not ready, not yet fit to lead men victoriously, and he bore it hard, the responsibility of lives lost, of a cause temporarily broken. He discovered the reasons in the narrow sectarianism, the opportunism of the Balkan Socialist movement, and he worked on himself till he was free of those vices, till he felt himself *Bolshevized*, reinforced with the experience of Lenin and the working class of Russia.

"I admit that my tone is hard and sharp," he told the judge. "The struggle of my life has been hard and sharp. My tone is frank and open. I seek to call things by their correct names. . . . I am defending myself, an accused Communist; I am defending my political honour, my honour as a revolutionary; I am defending my Communist ideology, my ideals, the content and significance of my whole life."

After the trial the three Bulgarian prisoners met in a common cell for the first time and Dimitrov summed up the struggle they had made. "There were four of us, Communists—four armed fighters. Torgler is a deserter, for he threw down his rifle and ran from the field of battle. You two did not throw down your rifles, you remained in position, but you did not shoot, and I had to shoot alone all the time." He shot alone, but his fire was strong enough to subdue the enemy's and finally to rout him. To the writer he must always be the symbol of man's spirit victorious against man's enemies. He is man alive.

CHAPTER XI

THE LOST ART OF PROSE

IT will doubtless only appear a platitude to remind the reader that to write the imaginative history of a man is to give oneself to the most difficult of all tasks, that of artistic creation. Your aspiring novelist may be greatly taken with the character of Dimitrov and those tremendous days at Leipzig, yet it will not help him at all if he believes that he can write a novel upon them by mere lively description of persons and events. No, a novel is history only in so far as it is the story of men in being, developing, living and perhaps dying. It has no relation at all to the writing of actual history, where surmise has no place, where all is collation, analysis and accurate generalization from observed facts.

To write imaginatively of Dimitrov you must first do away with the real Dimitrov who lives in Moscow and has an office in the building of the Communist International. You have to start, as it were, with a blank sheet and create an entirely new Dimitrov of the imagination, who is at once greater and less than the real man, greater because, if you are a good writer, your imagination will exalt as well as transform your vision of him, less, because you will never succeed in re-creating exactly as he was the man of flesh and blood, with all his physical characteristics, his quickness of mind, his faults and his virtues. Of course, despite that necessary blank sheet, you will nevertheless be grappling with a reality and the result you achieve must in the end depend upon the keenness of your perception of that reality. If it has not been sharp, intense, possessed almost of the quality of revelation (but not quite revelation, for that implies a certain absence of thought) you will never succeed in making your readers live through your experience of Dimitrov with the emotion needed to make him live again in *their* eyes. You have to force your experience on to other people, to transmit your perception of life to them, and to do that you must have mastered completely the reality with which your genius has contended.

If you are a very great writer indeed the result will be like the creation of a new world in which your character Dimitrov will appear to live a life of his own, independent of time and space. Yet in a sense that character is not yours at all, it is something you have torn away from life and re-created on the blank sheet, impelled by the strength and intensity of your experience. In accordance with your mastery of your materials, the more permanent will appear the result, the more splendid the reflection in it of life, of reality.

Dimitrov, however, for all you may have created a picture of a man who will live with the same timeless life as Don Quixote, Tom Jones, Anna Karenina or Julien Sorel, will be none the less the Communist printer who alone defied the blood-crazed rulers of the greatest despotism of our time. He will have arisen out of the struggle of classes and the clash of ideas reflecting that struggle. In order that you may create such a picture, in order to bring that embodiment of certain seemingly timeless features of the human spirit into relation with the actual forces which made possible his growth and his triumph, you have to possess certain artistic weapons.

In an earlier chapter I have quoted a phrase of Flaubert's which suggests, quite rightly in its context, that the greatest writers are those who have apparently the most consistently ignored the purely formal side of their art. It would nevertheless be as dangerous as foolish to draw from that the conclusion that the formal side is unimportant. Actually, these great writers were complete

masters of their craft, and if they often seem to break all
the rules it is only because their creative genius had to
make other rules to fit the grandeur of their imagination.
It is completely foreign to the spirit of Marxism to neglect
the formal side of art. To Marx form and content were
inextricably connected, inter-related by the dialectic of
life, and for the novelist of Socialist realism formal
questions are of first importance.

Take, for example, the question of "atmosphere." This
is that delicate relationship between character and en-
vironment, so difficult to obtain, which is essential to the
author if he is to heighten the reality of his characters,
give that intensity to the decisive moments of his work
which the action demands. It is precisely, indeed, the
quality which is lacking from the majority of novels on
social themes. Certainly, the attitude of the Socialist
writer to atmosphere can hardly be the same as that of
the realist of the older school, but he cannot ignore it
and he can learn a great deal from the writers of the past
as well as from the best novelists of the present as to the
means by which atmosphere is created. Among modern
writers, Faulkner, for example, is a master in the creation
of atmosphere, so that the atmosphere of terror, madness
or fear, will sometimes completely dominate his books,
almost overwhelming the characters. The very air will
breathe terror if Faulkner needs terror, it is often one of
his faults that he falls, in this respect, into some of the
worst traps of romantic writing.

It is not thus, however, that we should conceive of
character and environment, as being two separate things,
parallel, but unconnected, unchanging in their relations
throughout the action of the book. To make clear my
meaning, let us go back to our story of Dimitrov. This
novel is unthinkable without atmosphere. First, the at-
mosphere of Berlin after the *coup d'état*, the great city half
crazy with fear and suspicion, with the half-expressed,

the half-concealed; the very sounds and lights in the life of a modern town, the wheels of the traffic, the roar of the underground trains, the whirl and flash of the coloured street signs, would all be woven into this sinister symphony of hysteria and dread and uneasy expectation. It is on that background your characters would first appear, till the whole scene, perhaps, merged into the approach of Dimitrov in the Munich train, in the early morning, talking quietly to the woman passenger in his compartment, the buying of the paper with the news of the Reichstag fire, and his walking out of the station into the city where his enemies were already waiting for him, maddened by their own arson, hardly sure themselves of the reality of their acts.

From such a city the transition to the prison cell, the symbol of the new order, comes naturally. You have still the same atmosphere, but more concentrated, and in the centre is your little group of four "Communist soldiers." And here the artist would have to try, very subtly, to show the atmosphere changing, since from the darkness, brutality and terror which he abstracted out of the first scene into the second, something new would have to come as the figure of Dimitrov fighting against his enemies gradually began to dominate. The change from prison to battleground, he would have to show that in his "atmosphere."

Then last of all, the trial, the law-court being the stage where all the fantastic underworld from the city of the first scene appears to confront the four soldiers in the dock. And the different reactions of each soldier to this atmosphere, until again one of them enforces his will upon it, changes it, brings in light and air as the spirit of man asserts itself. All the time, though, the novelist would have to remember that underneath the solemn court, with its learned judges, smart policemen, cynical lawyers and eager pressmen, are the prison-cells, where the prisoners return after each session, whither Dimitrov was hustled each time he was expelled from court. He would have to control his "atmosphere" so perfectly that the end of the book would seem, quite naturally, to be like that of Beethoven's ninth symphony. The voices of human liberation would break down court walls and prison in their triumphant hymn to life.

The French essayist Alain, in his *Système des Beaux-Arts*, has a passage showing exactly the place of this *descriptive* writing in the novel: "One might say that the two methods of prose are thought and narration. It is by them that the objects hold together and the sentiments take form. In short, description should be supported, and it is the novelist's art not to construct his landscapes and houses without thoughts, as also he should not bring to sentiments and to actions edifices too great for them. In this sense Balzac's descriptions promise much, but not too much. The first comment to make upon these preparations, is that all their parts are connected by judgments; it is in this way that prose builds up. You would say that thought seeks there a hold everywhere; whereas poetry sufficiently describes through juxtaposition, because the rhythm holds us. This description must then be science in every one of its parts, so that the judgment binds one part to another; and, in this connection, you might usefully contrast the descriptive analyses of Balzac or of Stendhal with so many literary paintings, such as that of Carthage in *Salammbo*, which only betray the appearance of things. Every prose edifice holds together by thought in the first place. Thus are moving images held together or grouped around a centre. You might here venture to say that it is thought which makes body and matter. If the reader resists, it is because by thought he means abstract formulas which, in fact, grip nothing. And for all that it is true that Balzac or Stendhal have a better understanding of what a town like Alençon or Verrières is like than any geographer has been able to make us have.

"It is a thing worth noting that imagination at first does not enter into play in these descriptions; they seem a little abstract; you only see the judgments in them. It is afterwards, in the narration, that things are shown, not as displayed for a spectacle, but as they gather, appear and disappear around the man who is acting."

The raw material in which the writer works to express his thoughts on men and women is words. As he thinks, he writes, and the logical sequence of his thoughts expresses itself in the ordered form of dialogue and sentences. Much has been written about style, prose rhythms, "pattern" in prose, and so on. I do not propose to add to it, beyond suggesting perhaps another obvious platitude, that there is no living style where this conformity of word and thought is absent, that the romantic thought will demand a romantic style and the realist thought, the plain "prose" thought, a simple, realistic style. Few things are more irritating than the attempt deliberately to create style, or to produce ornament as a substitute for thought. Unfortunately, it has to be recognized that in times when thought becomes difficult, painful or unpleasant, then the affected style is likely to predominate. A more excellent example of this truth (which like the articles of the American Constitution, we hold to be self-evident) could not be found than in the modern "art" of biography which is all affectation without thought, and therefore "stylized" to the most absurd degree.

The greatest treasure-house of expression is to be found in the folk language of any people. Nor can this language ever be said to have died, though it constantly modifies itself. You could very well say of the greatest authors that it is difficult to judge whether they have actually created proverbial language or whether they merely used proverbial language. From Chaucer, through Shakespeare to Shaw, however, it is this popular, almost proverbial language on which our greatest authors have chiefly drawn. The academic critic and literary historian has made it almost a commonplace that the English version of the Bible is the source of language for almost all our great prose literature. Yet no one has ever, so far as I know, studied to find how much that version was merely the ordinary speech of English folk in the Elizabethan age. Certainly the language of the Bible has ever since remained very much the language of the common people, forming together with that of Milton and the *Pilgrim's Progress*, their literary inheritance to an extent the upper classes in our country could never claim.

This richness of speech and expression has suffered in our own century, but that its vitality is being renewed, partly by importation from America, partly by experience of life, there is little doubt. Much of the paleness and anaemia of our modern writing is due to the fact that many intellectuals have deliberately cut themselves off from this eternal spring of renewal, so that of modern writers one of the few whose prose has had real vitality (whatever we may think of him for other reasons) has been Kipling. Kipling soaked himself in the folk speech of England and America, nor was he ever afraid to seize on its latest and most modern manifestations in the new popular mythology growing up around the development of power machinery. The art of writing good prose is largely the lost one of calling things by their right names, the power which gave such force to Dimitrov's speech from the dock. It is a fact, a stubborn, awkward fact, that almost the only people in our country who still possess this ability, because they still have the necessary experience of life and store of words to which they add continually, are working people. Many American authors have recognized this in their own country, with the result that, for all their faults, the productions of the so-called "hard-boiled" school have created something much more like a living art and a living style than our English writers possess.

The last English writer to whom the art of calling things by their right names came almost as second nature was that remarkable working man William Cobbett, "the most conservative and the most radical man in Great Britain—the truest incarnation of Old England and the boldest progenitor of Young England," as Marx called him. Perhaps the reader will excuse two examples of this prose whose virtue was its ability to find the right names for things. They are from Cobbett's description of Lincolnshire:

"There is one deficiency, and that, with me, a great one, throughout this country of corn and grass and oxen and sheep, that I have come over during the last three weeks; namely, the want of *singing-birds*. We are now just in that season when they sing most. Here, in all this country, I have seen and heard only about four sky-larks, and not one other singing bird of any description, and of the small birds that do not sing I have seen only one *yellow-hammer*, and it was perched on the rail of a pound between Boston and Sibsey. Oh! the thousands of linnets all singing together on one tree in the sand-hills of Surrey! Oh! the carolling in the coppices and the dingles of Hampshire and Sussex and Kent! At this moment (five o'clock in the morning) the groves at Barn-Elm are echoing with the warblings of thousands upon thousands of birds. The *thrush* begins a little before it is light; next the *blackbird*; next the *larks* begin to rise; all the rest begin the moment the sun gives the signal; and from the hedges, the bushes, from the middle and the topmost twigs of the trees, comes the singing of endless variety; from the long dead grass comes the sound of the sweet and soft voice of the *white-throat* or *nettle-tern*, while the loud and merry song of the *lark* (the songster out of sight) seems to descend from the skies."

When Cobbett describes the country through which he rides he shows the very shape and texture of the earth, but he never describes any part of his English scene, birds singing, the Lincolnshire wolds, a farmers' meeting in a country playhouse, a Yorkshire horse-fair, without the consciousness that these things are part of man's life, and that they can only take their beauty, their meaning in relation to man's life. It is this that separates him from nature writers of the type of Hudson and Jeffries. Cobbett's English is sprung from Cobbett's England.

"When I was at St. Ives, in Huntingdonshire, an open country, I sat with the farmers, and smoked a pipe by way of preparation for evening service, which I performed on a carpenter's bench in a wheelwright's shop; my friends, the players, never having gained any regular settlement in that grand mart for four-legged fat meat, coming from the Fens, and bound to the Wen. While we were sitting, a hand-bill was handed round the table advertising *farming stock* for sale; and amongst the implements of husbandry 'an excellent fire-engine, several steel-traps, and spring-guns!' And that is the life, is it, of an English *farmer*? I walked on about six miles of the road from Holbeach to Boston. I have before observed upon the inexhaustible riches of this land. At the end of about five miles and three-quarters I came to a public-house, and thought I would get some breakfast; but the poor woman, with a tribe of children about her, had not a morsel of either meat or bread! At a house called an inn, a ·little further on, the landlord had no meat except a little bit of chine of bacon; and though there were a good many houses near the spot, the landlord told me that the people were become so poor that the butchers had left off killing meat in the neighbourhood. Just the

state of things that existed in France on the eve of the
Revolution. On that very spot I looked round me and
counted more than two thousand fat sheep in the pastures!
How long, how long, good God! is this state of things to
last? How long will these people starve in the midst of
plenty? How long will fire-engines, steel-traps, and
spring-guns be, in such a state of things, a protection to
property?"

Cobbett, I am greatly afraid, was not a pure artist,
but he wrote in a language which approaches uncom-
monly near to pure prose, wherein the connection between
word and idea is so completely happy as to appear to
the reader quite unquestionable. That is how it was.
This art of prose is a dying one in our own day, for in
order to call things by their right names, you must not
be afraid of the things you have to describe, nor allow
any barriers to arise between you and them. Cobbett's
idea of prose was one thing, the B.B.C.'s is another.
Cobbett used language to express life, the B.B.C. uses
it to conceal life.* In the English accents of the soldier-
farmer there is warmth, and passion, and the voice of
sense (as well as of that common sense which is really
only a familiar communion with the common things of
our life).

In the thin speech of the gentlemen of Portland Place
there are no feelings, passions, thoughts or sense-impres-
sions, no reflections of the loving and familiar things of
life, but only pale reflections of the ghosts and hobgoblins
that are substitutes for them in the minds of our modern
rulers. Perhaps it is unfair to make this comparison.
Perhaps, indeed; though it is such a melancholy fact
that from the time of Cobbett to our own day, the evolu-

---

* I refer particularly to that extraordinary list of subjects which
cannot be mentioned and words that cannot be used which is the
B.B.C.'s guide through life. The same list of prohibitions exists in
most newspaper offices.

tion of our language has been towards this bloodless, blameless ideal of the B.B.C., an evolution conditioned by the fear of the truth of life that is the most striking feature of the intellectual existence of our class society. If we are to start to call things by their names again, we shall have a lot of leeway to make up, a most indecent dog-fight to engage in with the literary pundits, by the side of which Victor Hugo's and Keats's battles will appear puny indeed, and we must strain our inventive and creative faculties to the utmost in our effort to give our language the new blood it demands. It may be that here the poets will take the lead. If so, then welcome, and let us go into the fight together encouraged by the thought that the fate of our language and the struggles to develop it, have in the past always been most closely bound up with the struggles of our country for national salvation.

CHAPTER XII

THE CULTURAL HERITAGE

THE relation between an author and the public is a peculiar and complicated one, something much more than that of simply author and reader. For the public is made up of all kinds of men and women of different classes, varying interests, passions and degrees of intelligence. The public is swayed (for all its apparent indifference, even supineness) by tremendous conflicts of class, by national and racial prejudices, by the inheritance of history working out its inevitable course in the life of humanity. From the public the author takes his characters as well as finds his readers there. Here he discovers both his raw material and his critics. In the greatest novels there is a kind of living unity between creator, characters and readers. Where that unity is wanting, where the author is aloof from his public, ignores it, or is spiritually ignorant of it, there is very likely to result an anaemia, a lack of some important element in the chemistry of imagination, which impoverishes the author's thought or cripples his powers. Not always, or necessarily so, of course, for Stendhal we know consciously wrote for a public yet unborn, accepted that he would be neither understood nor appreciated by his own generation.

Now the author, though in private life he may be the most timid and indecisive of mortals, in his relation to the public as the object of his art must be a mixture of Henry II and Tamerlane, a ruthless master and conqueror, bending all to his own will. Yet it follows also that even the most absolute tyrant cannot be a real master, a maker of history, unless he understands history, unless he possesses a keen sympathy for the unseen processes that mould men's lives. So the author must know his people, be as familiar with them as though the men were his constant tavern companions, the women his loving doxies and the children his own brats. History's most picturesque tyrants, men who ruled in a god-like isolation, have always (in legend) mingled at night-time with their subjects, carefully disguised as common men. The author who cannot do the same is condemned from the start to impotence or, should he insist on making a nuisance of himself in print by presenting a false view of life, to the contempt with which history regards the unsuccessful despot.

For this creative communion to be completely effectual, sympathy is not enough. Or, rather, the sympathy of the author must be informed by history, he must be able to use the cultural heritage of his nation, as the people itself is able to use the political heritage.* The two are,

---

* Mr. T. S. Eliot, in *The Sacred Wood*, has some interesting arguments on this question of tradition and heritage with which I cannot altogether agree. He suggests that the writer must have an historical sense compelling him to write "not merely with his own generation in his bones but with a feeling that the whole of the literature of Europe from Homer and within it the whole of the literature of his own country has a simultaneous existence and composes a simultaneous order."

This is only a partial truth. For the past has no meaning outside the present, and every present has its own judgment of the past. It is the way in which this judgment is formed which should be the most important concern of the critic. However, Mr. Eliot shows his own view of tradition to be essentially a passive one. "No poet, no artist of any art, has his complete meaning alone. His significance, his appreciation is the appreciation of his relation to the dead poets and arts. You cannot value him alone; you must set him, for contrast and comparison, among the dead."

Surely this is a scurvy treatment of both past and present. If there is an organic connection between the two it is not this of "contrast and comparison." Truly we judge every poet as part of a whole, but not as that part which is merely passively conditioned by his heritage. The poet or novelist is not an inheritor of dead property. He makes

in fact, closely interwoven. A people cannot play its part in history if it renounces its cultural past, any more than if it renounces its political past. A writer who inherits from the culture of the past only pale aesthetic ghosts and not a living body of tradition will betray his own cause. So it happens also, as I have insisted throughout this essay, that the greatest writers are not men who are indifferent to the active life of their times. Shakespeare in his historical plays was a keen politician. Milton, besides writing the epic of the struggle of good and evil, took a part in the greatest revolution of our history and in his prose works developed political principles that his countrymen will ignore at their peril. Fielding the magistrate was a defender of the poor and oppressed, a reformer of a brutal legal system. Byron, first and greatest of the romantic poets, delivered the speech to the Lords upon the Luddites besides writing *Childe Harold*. "There is a spiritual community binding together the living and the dead," wrote Wordsworth; "the good, the brave, and the wise, of all ages. We would not be rejected from this community."

Milton in his speech to the Parliament of England "for

use of the past in order to change, not only the past itself (by his personal achievement), but also the present. Culture is something we must use in order to live, and not merely an object of aesthetic contemplation.

Mr. Eliot, indeed, partly understands this, for in his preface he admits that in preferring Dante to Shakespeare he has to view culture as such an active agent in life that here morals, religion and politics are also concerned. Each new work, Mr. Eliot argues in his essay on "Tradition," alters, ever so slightly, the whole existing order of past work. True, but what are the forces behind this alteration? How does the change take place?

We judge the past as our own life compels us to judge, our life conditioned, not only by our heredity, but also by the class struggles, the passions of our own time. Each new work makes its change conditioned by these same forces. We cannot see only the past. We must see first the present, which is always in process of change.

the liberty of unlicensed printing" in words which are a part of England, described what is the noblest heritage of our race:

"If it be desired to know the immediate cause of all this free writing and free speaking, there cannot be assigned a truer than your own mild and free, and humane government; it is the liberty, Lords and Commons, which your own valorous and happy counsels have purchased us, liberty which is the nurse of all great wits; this is that which hath rarefied and enlightened our spirits like the influence of Heaven; this is that which hath enfranchized, enlarged and lifted up our apprehensions degrees above themselves. Ye cannot make us now less capable, less knowing, less eagerly pursuing of the truth, unless ye first make yourselves, that made us so, less the lovers, less the founders of our true liberty. We can grow ignorant again, brutish, formal and slavish, as ye found us; but you then must first become that which ye cannot be, oppressive, arbitrary and tyrannous, as they were from whom ye have freed us. That our hearts are now more capacious, our thoughts more erected to the search and expectation of greatest and exactest things, is the issue of your own virtue propagated in us; ye cannot suppress that unless ye reinforce an abrogated and merciless law, that fathers may dispatch at will their own children. And who shall then stick closest to ye, and excite others? not he who takes up arms for coat and conduct, and his four nobles of Danegelt. Although I dispraise not the defence of just immunities, yet love my peace better, if that were all. Give me the liberty to know, to utter, and to argue freely according to conscience above all liberties."

Liberty did not spring fully armed into the world, like the goddess Athene. It is a slow and painful growth of history, of many stages, bringing with it many revolutions and abrupt changes. Milton spoke at one crisis in our history when freedom took a great leap, a crisis when the selfishness and bigotry of one form of property had to be broken, because it was a fetter on our material progress as well as on our minds. The selfishness of the man who took up arms "for coat and conduct, and his four nobles of Danegelt" has been broken, but in turn another form of property, of ignoble egotism, has taken its place, and in our day is proving a bar to our progress, a shackle on our minds which threatens the further development of our heritage of liberty. We have grown as a nation since Milton's day, and our England is a very different country. But the time has now come when Milton's descendants are being forced to recognize that economic slavery and national decay are bound up with one another. If the nation is to live, liberty must take another leap forward.

At the risk of appearing to preach a political lesson which on the surface may seem to be but little connected with my central theme, I will remind my readers of two most unhappy episodes in our history which have taken place in this year, 1936, and ask them to consider their deepest import in our national life. In doing so they will, I believe, understand that there is a very real connection between such political events and the content of our national vision, which in turn must colour the writer's imagination.

In 1936 the Government of Britain, having in its care the fortunes of our people and the inheritance of our nation, has been drawn into two unfortunate conflicts in which foreign imperialist interests have threatened the imperial interests of Britain. The first of these was the Italian adventure in Abyssinia, in which the British Government, having first irresolutely opposed, finally shamefully acquiesced in, the rape of a friendly country, thereby allowing the Fascist tyranny in Italy to establish a great Power in the Eastern Mediterranean athwart the communications of Britain to the East. In the second case, when a group of generals and unprincipled Fascist reactionaries, having risen in revolt against the lawful and democratic Government of Spain, threatened that country's independence (by help received at a price from German and Italian reaction) and her recently acquired liberty, our Government again, hesitatingly and un-decidedly, threw its weight rather on the side of reaction than of liberty, thereby making possible the establishment of aggressive German and Italian imperialism at the Western gate of the Mediterranean.

In each case, the Government, moved by a narrow class instinct which brings it nearer in sympathy to foreign tyranny than its own democratic people at home has acted against the national interest and eventually against even the imperial interest of the small class of great property owners whom it represents (though this is not to say that the national interest is identical with that of imperialism—far from it). The events in Spain might have been supposed to have stirred historic memories in English minds. On the colours of our regiments are the names of Salamanca, Badajoz, Vittoria, Albuera, Tala-vera and many other towns and villages of that Iberian peninsula soaked in British blood. The greatest sea fight in our history was decided off Cape Trafalgar. The greatest military campaign waged by British arms, the last campaign in our history in which we had both victory and glory, in which courage and military genius were shown in equal proportions, was for the establish-ment of Spanish independence against a bold, unscrupu-lous tyranny. In the ranks of the Spanish volunteers who fought so bravely with us, were Spanish Jacobins, revolutionaries.

The poet Wordsworth with the insight of imaginative genius saw that this war, both for Britain and for Spain, was a national war, a war of the whole people against the abominable, inhuman idea that a State might exist where "at the head of all is the mind of one man who acts avowedly upon the principle that everything which can be done safely by the supreme power of a State may be done" (Tract on the Convention of Cintra). With the same insight Wordsworth noted that the war against France begun in 1793, like the war against the independence of the American States which preceded it, was a wrongful war, against the national interest, in which the Government was concerned only with the narrow class interest of the oligarchy that it represented.

When Napoleon, from being a vital, revolutionary force, smashing the bonds of feudalism throughout Europe, became, by the dialectic of history, the ally and protector of these same feudal forces, when, from being a national liberator, he became an oppressor of the liberty of other nations, the war against him became a just and necessary one and his own defeat inevitable.

Our own bourgeoisie, from the Tudors to the end of the nineteenth century, fulfilled a progressive role in history, developing the productive forces of our country, creating a great literature and a great science, influencing the growth of other nations in Europe, and being in turn influenced by them. In general, its class interests and the national interests coincided. When they did not, when the greed of property, the incompetence of a corrupt and narrow oligarchy, blinded them, the result was usually national disaster, as in the American war and the first years of the war against revolutionary France. The energy and courage of the handful of people in our tiny island, led by this bourgeoisie and our bourgeois-minded aristocracy, built up an immense Empire. They used abominable cruelties to achieve this, and set up in the countries they conquered tyrannies which would never have been tolerated at home, in order that they might compel their subject nations to pay tribute to this victorious English middle-class and their aristocratic allies. But even here their part was a progressive one, though not in the sense in which the apologists of British rule in India now use that word.

Marx has described this revolutionary side of British colonial rule in unforgettable words, which I will quote at some length, for later it will be necessary to point out that in the relations between our country and the East, there must also be found important elements which are needed for creating that new imagination so necessary for the refertilizing of our national genius. Referring to the effects of British rule in India, Marx wrote: "English interference having placed the spinner in Lancashire and the weaver in Bengal, or sweeping away both Hindoo spinner and weaver, dissolved these small semi-barbarian, semi-civilized communities, by blowing up their economical bases, and thus produced the greatest and, to speak the truth, the only *social* revolution ever heard of in Asia. . . . England, it is true, in causing a social revolution in Hindostan, was actuated only by the vilest interests, and was stupid in her manner of enforcing them. But that is not the question. The question is, can mankind fulfil its destiny without a fundamental revolution in the social state of Asia? If not, whatever may have been the crimes of England, she was the unconscious tool of history in bringing about that revolution."

In a sequel to this article, Marx developed his thought further: "All the English *bourgeoisie* may be forced to do will neither emancipate nor materially mend the social condition of the mass of the people, depending not only on the development of the productive powers, but of their appropriation by the people. But what they will not fail to do is to lay down the material premises for both. Has the bourgeoisie ever done more? Has it ever affected a progress without dragging individuals and people through blood and dirt, through misery and degradation? The Indians will not reap the fruits of the new elements of society scattered among them by the British bourgeoisie till in Great Britain itself the now ruling classes shall have been supplanted by the industrial proletariat, or till the Hindoos themselves shall have grown strong enough to throw off the English yoke altogether."

We can understand the humiliations of our ,Government's policy in Africa and Spain, if we bear in mind these prophetic words of Marx. Torn between a desire to defend its Indian possessions, from which it draws so much of its economic power, and its natural sympathy for the enemies of human progress among the Fascist terrorists of Germany and Italy, our ruling class, its progressive mission in the world long ago exhausted, is feeble and hesitating to a criminal degree, sets itself apart from the interest of the British peoples as a whole and even jeopardizes our existing liberties and national independence, all the virtue that our fathers propagated in us, to recall Milton's noble words. They are now, indeed, in the very position which Milton declared the enemies of liberty must take up, of reinforcing "an abrogated and merciless law, that fathers may despatch their own children."

The immense possessions of our decaying rulers are the envy of other Powers more unscrupulous and tyrannical even than themselves, Powers who have reached the ultimate point of decay by denying their own national heritage along with the common human heritage of culture. To defend these possessions our rulers must make common cause with democracy and progress against Fascism and reaction. But that, they rightly argue, is in the end to hazard them still more certainly by raising up the enemies of their privilege at home. So they seek, with fumbling hesitation, for a compromise which will save them nothing and jeopardize more important human rights than the right of a British bank, insurance company or industrial monopoly, to maintain its robber power in India, Africa or Western Asia.

To-day the interest of our people, the true national interest, is in supporting the freedom of the great movements for democracy and national liberty which are re-vitalizing the Arabian, African and Indian peoples. An alliance of free peoples will prove a stronger guard for the liberties of all, including our own, than the present effort to maintain an Imperial tyranny which is a menace to our own independence as a nation because of the very inability of the ruling Imperial clique to defend the Juggernaut they have created. That Juggernaut will crush them beneath its weight. Unless we understand our position and hold out the friendly hand of a free England to a free India, Africa and Arabistan, it will crush us also.

Why have I dwelt in such detail on a political question? Because with the proper solution of this question is bound up the artistic question which is the subject of my essay. Our fate as a people is being decided to-day. It is our fortune to have been born at one of those moments in history which demand from each one of us as an individual that he make his private decision. Hamlet could bemoan his fate in being born at such a juncture, and we also would wish for a more peaceful time, but we, no more than Hamlet, can escape from making our decision. We are a part of that spiritual community with the dead of which Wordsworth spoke, we cannot stand aside, and by our actions we shall extend our imagination, because we shall have been true to the passions in us.

There is being performed in London as I write a play by a famous Austrian dramatist, Arthur Schnitzler, on the subject of anti-Semitism. The play, Mr. Desmond MacCarthy in a penetrating review has pointed out, is old-fashioned, and the author, moreover, is dead. But the theme is very much alive, more than ever it was in the author's lifetime, and the play is only old-fashioned, as Mr. MacCarthy curiously but truly says, because "the construction is the kind exactly suited to the sort of play it is, which happens to be one seldom written to-day, because the dramatists who know their job best don't know what to think of life themselves and, therefore, very properly don't try to write plays intended to make people think."

The artist does not know what to think of life. Yet the artist cannot create life unless he dares to think about life. He may make a little picture of unimportant people, or he may dissect a harmless emotion very nicely, but he will not create life without thought. "I think, therefore I am," has its meaning for art as well as for life. Alain, the French essayist, has shrewdly observed that the chief fault of contemporary psychology is to have believed too much in the mad and the sick. It is part of the general fear of life, the effort to keep out of the community of humanity. "We would not be rejected from this community," was Wordsworth's conclusion: "And therefore do we hope." Hope will return on that condition alone, that we are not rejected from the community.

The modern novelist, accepting the primary error of the modern psychologist, tries to find a basis for his imagination in the mad and the sick, having no hope, or lacking the courage to seek a basis for hope. This is as true of Mr. Evelyn Waugh, whose acceptance of this basis leads him to the obscurantist pessimism of the Roman Church, as it is of Mr. Aldous Huxley, who from the same basis preaches a negative pacifist anarchy, a negation of all action which in practise is little different from Mr. Waugh's renunciation of the world and its sins. "The sword," thought Wordsworth, "in the hands of the good and the virtuous, is the most intelligible symbol of abhorrence." Aldous Huxley, being unable to decide between good and evil, since that demands a view of human life not based on the mad and the sick, abhors the symbol of abhorrence more than he does evil itself.

To-day, the Russian Revolution, proclaiming that it is possible to organize human life without the oppression and exploitation of man by man, on the foundation of the friendly co-operation of free and equal peoples, has given us the nourishment for lack of which our modern imagination has been languishing. It is in this that the importance of Soviet literature, though still so young and imperfect, lies. It has shown us how we can again draw fresh strength from the unquenchable sources of our own energy, our *liberty* which is the issue of the virtue propagated in us by our fathers, the liberty to make man what he must be, "the sovereign of circumstances," as Marx called him.

Wordsworth was conscious of the same impelling force giving strength to the imagination of his time from the source of the French Revolution. "Great was it in that dawn to be alive," and the greatness of the dawn first gave his eyes the fresh vision of the "Lyrical Ballads." The vision faded somewhat in Wordsworth during the weary years of struggle afterwards, but it revived with the rise of the national revolution in Spain and the passion which that revolt stirred in the English people. It inspired in him one of the sublimest pieces of English prose in the *Tract on the Convention of Cintra*. In the Tract he uncovers the real basis of poetic imagination, the true relation between man's vision and man's life:

"Oppression, its own blind and predestined enemy, has poured this of blessedness upon Spain—that the enormity of the outrages, of which she has been the victim, has created an object of love and of hatred—of apprehensions and of wishes—adequate (if that be possible) to the utmost demands of the human spirit. The heart that serves in this cause, if it languish, must languish from its own constitutional weakness; and not through want of nourishment from without. But it is a belief propagated in books, and which passes currently among talking men as part of their familiar wisdom, that the hearts of the many *are* constitutionally weak; that they *do* languish; and are slow to answer to the requisitions of things. I entreat those, who are in this delusion, to look behind them and about them for the evidence of experience. Now this, rightly understood, not only gives no support to any such belief; but proves that the truth is in direct opposition to it. The history of all ages; tumults after tumults; wars, foreign or civil, with short or with no breathing-spaces, from generation to generation; wars— why and wherefore? Yet with courage, with perseverance, with self-sacrifice, with enthusiasm—with cruelty driving forward the cruel man from its own terrible nakedness, and attracting the more benign by the accompaniment of some shadow which seems to sanctify it; the senseless weaving and interweaving of factions—vanishing and re-viving and piercing each other like the Northern Lights; public commotions, and those in the bosom of the indi-vidual; the long calenture to which the Lover is subject; the blast, like the blast of the desert, which sweeps perennially through a frightful solitude of its own making in the mind of the Gamester; the slowly quickening but ever-quickening descent of appetite down which the Miser is propelled; the agony and cleaving oppression of grief; the ghost-like hauntings of shame; the incubus of revenge; the life-distemper of ambition; these inward existences, and the visible and familiar occurrences of daily life in every town and village; the patient curiosity and contagious acclamations of the multitude in the streets of the city and within the walls of the theatre; a procession, or a rural dance; a hunting, or a horse-race; a flood, or a fire; rejoicing and ringing of bells for an unexpected gift of good fortune, or the coming of a foolish heir to his estate; . . . these demonstrate incontestibly that the passions of men (I mean, the soul of sensibility in the heart of man)—in all quarrels, in all contests, in all quests, in all delights, in all employments which are either sought by men or thrust upon them—do immeasurably transcend their objects. The true sorrow of humanity consists in this: not that the mind of man fails; but that the course and demands of action and of life so rarely correspond with the dignity and intensity of human desires; and hence that, which is slow to languish, is too easily turned aside and abused."

Wordsworth's view of the relation between the imagination and life is the exact opposite of the view implicit in Mr. MacCarthy's criticism of Schnitzler and so widely held by modern writers. Wordsworth's view is a revolutionary one and a heroic one, for it is rooted in the belief that man is "the sovereign of circumstances," that the dignity and intensity of his desires can only find fulfilment by transcending themselves in action. There are rare occasions in history, in the personal history of each individual, in the common history of mankind, when the demands of life fully correspond with the dignity and intensity of man's desires. Such an occasion confronts us to-day when the conflict of classes throughout the world has "created an object of love and of hatred—of apprehensions and of wishes—adequate (if that be possible) to the utmost demands of the human spirit." The novelist who is able to understand this will rise like a giant above his times, re-create the epic art of modern civilization, and truly inherit the tradition of our English letters.

Those who follow closely the life of our sister-democracy in France will have noted the movement in intellectual life there taking place parallel with the political revival of the Republican spirit. The people of France, threatened in their national independence, all their priceless national heritage in danger, have rallied in a common front to maintain their liberties and to make their country free, strong and happy. This movement, taking its beginning from the welding into a common unity of the working people, and gradually spreading to include all those who live by their own labour, of whatever class, has drawn together the most diverse elements in French letters, particularly among the novelists. The Communist Malraux, the anarchist Céline, the liberal Jules Romains, the Socialist Bloch, the supreme individualist Gide, have managed to find a common ground. They have entered again into the communion of the people and are able, because that community has helped them to revive the great traditions of French letters, to find refreshment in it for their art. They have not any longer to submit to the supreme humiliation of the artist, attributed to the British dramatists by Mr. Desmond MacCarthy, of not knowing what to think about life.

There is one more element lacking, however, to make up that modern and revolutionary imagination which I conceive of as essential to the revival of the novel. It is the element of colour, fantasy and ironical vision which we have almost lost since the Renaissance. It came then from the East, for the discovery of the magical East, the passing of the caravans over the great deserts to China, the girdling of the globe by the navigators of England and of Portugal, brought about at that time a contact of civilizations which truly fired men's minds. That element I have in mind perhaps appears most clear in Cervantes, but you may find it in Shakespeare also.

This reinforcement of imagination must come to us again now that Asia is awaking from her long sleep, now that among these ancient and historic peoples a revolutionary assertion of their unquenchable vitality is taking place. The sentimental mourn the introduction of "Western" ideas to the East, by which they mean modern science and means of production. They need not mourn.

Once the peoples of Asia, who in part have already won their liberation, have mastered these, they will be no slavish imitators of our own weaknesses. Their co-operation will be found essential to the building of a new outlook on life, and it will not prove the least important part of that outlook. I mention the peoples of Asia, because their civilization is the oldest and strongest in the world, but neither should we overlook that the vision of a liberated humanity will be strengthened also by the almost untouched stores of energy in the African and in the Indo-Spanish peoples of America.

The world is divided hopelessly to-day. The forces of unification are, however, at work, and this the novelist of the new age has to bear ever first in his mind. The process of this unification has been so well described by Marx in the articles on India from which I have already quoted, that this essay cannot better close than on his conclusion to that analysis of the relations between East and West:

"The centralization of capital is essential to the exist-ence of capital as an independent power. The destructive influence of that centralization upon the markets of the world does but reveal, in the most gigantic dimensions, the inherent organic laws of political economy now at work in every civilized town. The bourgeois period of history has to create the material basis of the new world—on the one hand universal intercourse founded upon the mutual dependency of mankind, and the means of that intercourse; on the other hand the development of the productive powers of man and the transformation of material production into a scientific domination of natural agencies. Bourgeois industry and commerce create these material conditions of a new world in the same way as geological revolutions have created the surface of the earth. When a great social revolution shall have mastered the results of the bourgeois epoch, the market of the world and the modern powers of production, and sub-jected them to the common control of the most advanced peoples, then only will human progress cease to resemble that Hindoo pagan idol, who would not drink the nectar but from the skulls of the slain."

LITERATURE AND POLITICS

*A Speech at the Memorial Meeting for Maxim Gorki at the
Conway Hall, London, June,* 1936

THE death of Maxim Gorki who was, I think we must all
agree, one of the greatest of the imaginative writers of
our time, is something that has been felt as a very bitter
loss far outside the frontiers of his own country, the
U.S.S.R. Gorki himself was a man of such great courage,
of such deep simplicity and of such intense honesty that
he became loved not only in his own country but by
thousands of others, in all countries throughout the world,
who are fighting the same battle for humanity which
Gorki fought.

In England in the last months we have had three or
four writers, perhaps one or two *great* English writers,
who have died, and in whose honour no meetings have
been organized. But we are to-night paying honour to a
man who is by birth a foreigner to us. He was loved so
well outside his own country because in his work he
expressed sincerely the suffering and hope and will to
conquer of the exploited people in all parts of the world.
There are few men who fought against human baseness
with the energy and courage with which Gorki fought,
and there are few men who saw so clearly that the roots
of human baseness are to be found in the property
structure of our civilization.

In the last public speech Gorki ever made, referred to
to-night by Mr. Hubert Griffiths and Mr. Ralph Bates,
in opening the first Congress of the Union of Soviet
Writers, he said the following:

"We appear as the judges of a world condemned to perish, and as men who affirm a real humanism, a humanism of the revolutionary working class, a humanism of a people summoned by history to liberate the whole world of those who toil from envy, venality and all those vices which have for centuries distorted men who live by their labour.

"We are the enemies of property, the base and terrible Goddess of the capitalist world, we are the enemies of all the zoological individualism which is the declared religion of that Goddess."

Gorki's life appears to us to-day as a great and significant one because his life was bound up with the effort to dethrone that God. Gorki's life was bound up with the emergence of the Russian working class as a class for itself. Gorki's life was bound up very closely with the past of the working class in Russia, in a period unique in the history of the world, during which that class emerged to freedom and a new society was built up on a basis of no private property in the means of production, a society without classes, the first society wherein man has found his full value as a human being.

Gorki's life was bound up with the three revolutions in Russia: in 1905, in the February revolution of 1917, and the October revolution of 1917. It was mentioned to-night by many of the speakers that Gorki was a true and intimate friend of Lenin and Stalin. Like them he went through the period of prison and exile. From the beginning of Gorki's political life he was a supporter of the Bolsheviks. Gorki himself was a tramp, factory worker and rail worker, and took part in the life of the Russian working class. After a period of anarchism he saw in the Bolsheviks, and in the person of Lenin, the determination and simplicity and unconquerable faith which were going to overthrow the Empire of the Tsar, and Gorki summed up and described these qualities in the book of memoirs he wrote about Lenin. Gorki always felt that it was these qualities which were going to transform the Russian nation.

There is one problem which should interest us very deeply. How is it that Gorki, who came out of the depths of Russian society, became so famous overnight in the Russian literary world. I think that you can see why that is, if you look for a moment at the state of Russian society and literature at the time. Chekhov, then Russia's greatest writer, was a man who came out of the period of the terrible despair in the eighties. There seemed to be no future for the intellectuals; the best forces in Russian society seemed to have been sacrificed in a useless struggle against Tsardom, and all Chekhov's work is impregnated with this feeling. Tolstoi, at the time Gorki became famous, had already adopted a position of complete Christian negation. But Gorki brought something fresh to this despair and carried a new message of hope to the whole of the Russian people, and it is for this reason— because he came as a new force inside the life of the Russian nation, that overnight he became famous throughout Russia. You can feel it in the whole of his style.

No one has said anything about Gorki as a writer in the technical sense. Gorki has suffered from his translators into English, but Gorki as a Russian writer is full of a force which comes straight from the people among whom he lived. He always emphasized that the richest treasure house of language is to be found in the speech of the simple people, among the folk-lore and stories of the people—there is to be found the greatest enrichment of language and of literature. The whole of his own work is proof of this.

Gorki rapidly became famous and was elected a member of the Academy of Letters of the Russian Empire, and just as rapidly Gorki's name was removed at the direct command of the Tsar himself. As a protest against this disgraceful act of victimization, and to their ever-lasting honour, two of the greatest Russian writers also resigned from membership of the Academy—Chekhov and Korolenko. But what a picture it gives us of the state of literature in the early days of our century! That three of the greatest representatives of Russian literature should be forced to resign (one at least was removed) and that Tolstoi about the same time should have been suffering from ex-communication by the Orthodox Church, and had the anathema read against him in every place of worship in the Russian Empire! But Gorki showed the writers in Russia that if autocracy was brutal and violent there were ways and means of fighting the autocracy, that there was no reason to despair even after the terrible defeat of 1905. After this period Gorki went into emigration which lasted many years, but all the time he was abroad in the United States and elsewhere he was working for the Social-Democratic Party. When he went to live in Capri, Gorki carried on his fight for the overthrow of autocracy and for the coming of the Russian revolution.

You will remember that he started a school for the training of revolutionary workers at Capri. At the con-ference held last week-end of writers in London, H. G. Wells in a speech he made said something not very complimentary about the three tailors of Tooley Street who were settling the fate of the British Empire, and that remark met with a rebuke from Ilya Ehrenburg who mentioned that Gorki at one time in Capri did not think it beneath him to collect one metal worker, one tailor and one carpenter, and believed that these men might overthrow the Russian Empire, which seemed then as strong as the British Empire is to-day.

Gorki in this period did other things besides carrying on schools. He engaged in active revolutionary work.

Lenin's correspondence with Gorki is full of letters which deal not only with questions of philosophy but also deal with practical questions of how Gorki could help the Bolsheviks to smuggle their paper into Russia. He got in touch with the Italian Seamen's Union to take the Bolshevik literature into Odessa.

In the *Spectator* to-day I read a notice by Mr. E. H. Carr upon Gorki's work. In the course of that notice Carr said in the period of Capri Gorki unfortunately took to writing political novels, the very names of which to-day are forgotten. Those of you who are workers in this audience —have you forgotten the name of *Mother*? There are many people outside of Russia who have never forgotten that book. There are people all over the world who got their first introduction to politics through *Mother*. It is a unique distinction of this book that it also gave birth to another work of art—the great film of *Mother*.

This question of politics cannot be separated from the name of Gorki. In Tuesday's *Times* there was a leading article on the question of British authors. *The Times* does not often honour us. This time the leading article was to rebuke a certain section of British authors for having had the bad taste to make a poor joke by proposing that the Authors' Society should affiliate to the Trade Union Congress. What is the meaning of that resolution, which was unfortunately lost? A great many British authors to-day feel there is no future for English literature unless we can have a closer co-operation of writers and the working class. They feel this is the greatest safeguard for the heritage of British culture to-day. They feel it is the greatest hope for the future. Then again *The Times* this week has been devoting space to literature. On Thursday they reported a view upon literature in their columns. It was put forward by Mr. Charles Morgan, who is a collaborator of *The Times* and apparently believes that the writer should be entirely protected and cut off from his fellow men by the whole structure of our present society. He was presenting a prize to Mr. Evelyn Waugh and said: "He had seen such prizes sneered at, but sneers at the Hawthornden had always been based on the same complaint: that it was not administered by a literary or political clique. If they believed, as many people nowadays did honestly believe, that art was a waste of time unless it was used as an instrument of politics, then certainly they would not approve the Hawthornden committee. But in these days, when it had become true to say that among the great Powers of Europe, England and France alone permitted liberty of thought and speech, it was, he thought, of value that once à year they should be invited to honour a good book on its merits as a book and not because it had been written in subservience to some existing or hoped-for dictatorship—a book, moreover, with which, so far as its opinions were concerned, he himself, and perhaps certain members of the committee, were sometimes in political disagreement. That was as it should be."

It is perhaps due to ignorance that this view is advanced by Mr. Charles Morgan. He overlooks entirely the fact that in many cases literature is political, openly and deliberately political art. Look into the history of one country, into the history of Turkey. There was no dramatic literature at all in Turkey until the early seventies. The greatest Turkish poet of the nineteenth century wrote a play with a political aim in order to bring to the masses who could not read or write, the need to fight against the despotism in Turkey. This play started a whole new field of art in the life of the country. You can find the same thing happening in many countries time and time again. The art of the novel was founded in this country by a man who was extremely political in all his work, by Defoe, and his best known work, *Robinson Crusoe*, was actually used as a thesis in political economy by the supporters of the capitalist system in the eighteenth century.

The point I want to make is that to-day there are more and more writers who believe their only hope is to take the path which was first shown to us by Maxim Gorki, which will protect the best heritage of our country and fight for a new and better nation. We have had important writers who have sprung from the working class in our own country—H. G. Wells, Middleton Murry and D. H. Lawrence. These three came from working-class families but all three of these men have left the class from which they came. All three of these men tried to make their way into "society," and to-day in our country a writer can only do this by making a compromise and allowing himself to be taken up by the clique of aristocratic and plutocratic dealers in culture, who believe they possess a monopoly of our intellectual life. If you read the autobiographies of these three men you find there a terrible story of the fight which they have carried on against poverty and against snobbery, and you can see the tragedy of how in each case snobbery won. You can see here one of the most pathetic features of our intellectual life in the past two generations, the destruction of the cultural life in this country by the ruling class.

I think it is a great thing and a remarkable thing that young writers are renouncing the path taken by Wells, Lawrence and Middleton Murry. They are not going to allow this degenerate social clique to monopolize the intellectual life of our country.

The critics say that politics destroyed Gorki. They say, see what he did after 1917, meaning that he did nothing creative. Gorki's creative work since 1917, both in quality and quantity, would compare favourably with any other European writer's. His work in the social sense was a work which did greater honour to a name already certain of immortality, than anything he did before. Gorki prepared the way for a new culture which was bound to come with the establishment of socialism: his social work was essentially creative and not merely protective. Again, the work he has done since he finally returned to the Soviet Union in 1928; the tremendous task he undertook of reorganizing the whole of Russian literature, and forming the Soviet writers into one great Union of Writers, was something which must make him remembered with gratitude by every single writer in the country.

Ralph Bates has mentioned the original work Gorki did in sponsoring the collective writing of the *White Sea Canal*; but this is only one volume of an enormous work which was undertaken on Gorki's initiative—a work which is to be a history of all the factories and enterprises, of all the great farms in the Soviet Union, the work which will show the living building up of socialism. It is not meant to be a great literary work, it is meant to be a history of the building of socialism, and for the first time to make such a collective history the best creative forces in the country have been brought forward to assist. That is a tremendous work to the credit of Gorki. Again, Gorki was the man who first suggested, and first organized, the writing of the history of the Civil War, of the heroic period of the Russian Revolution, and in the first volume of this it is clear that Gorki and Stalin have collaborated in the writing of many chapters.

In closing I should like to mention two reactions towards the death of Gorki. The first reaction is the reaction of George Bernard Shaw. The message which Shaw sent to the Soviet Government was one of pessimism and defeat. Shaw said he felt that the old men were all dying off; there was little use for them to live any longer. Why worry about the big names in the past in the Soviet Union—they had the future to think of, but you cannot think of the future without the past and the past of Gorki was the past of the working class which made the revolution possible. The Soviet Union to-day is mourning a man they loved because they felt this so strongly.

The other reaction I had to the death of Gorki was a different one. It came from a London worker, a factory girl, who read the account of Gorki's funeral in the papers. She said, "It is sad to die when one is loved by so many people." That expressed something which was very true. It is sad for a man to die when he is so loved by the people; a man should live because he must see all these things he lived for come to birth; because those people with whom he is connected are all the time re-creating his own life.

There is also this to bear in mind, that this love which was shown to Gorki will be fertile for the future of the Soviet Union, will create many more and greater Maxim Gorkis for the first Socialist State, master engineers of the human soul.

SELECT BIBLIOGRAPHY

The following bibliography omits short contributions of Fox's to the *Sunday Worker*, the *Daily Worker*, the *Communist*, the *Communist Review*, and *Left Review*. In addition to the Preface to this volume, the bibliography *Marxism and Aesthetics* compiled by Lee Baxandall (Humanities Press, New York, 1968) contains helpful references to some of these. Unless stated otherwise place of publication is London.

"Social Changes as Seen in Literature," and "Literature and Life," *Plebs*, June 1922.

Captain Youth: A Romantic Comedy for all Socialist Children, C. W. Daniel, 1922.

People of the Steppes, Constable, 1925.

A Defence of Communism, in reply to H. J. Laski, Communist Party of Great Britain, 1927.

Storming Heaven, Constable, 1928.

Marx, Engels and Lenin on the Irish Revolution, Modern Books, London n.d. [1932]. Reissued as *Marx, Engels and Lenin on Ireland*, International Publishers, New York, 1940.

Lenin: A Biography, Gollancz, 1933.

The Colonial Policy of British Imperialism, Martin Lawrence, 1933.

The Class Struggle in Britain in the Epoch of Imperialism, two volumes (third volume never published), Martin Lawrence, n.d. [1933].

"The Relation of Literature to Dialectical Materialism," in *Aspects of Dialectical Materialism*, by H. Levy, John Macmurray, Ralph Fox, R. Page Arnot, J. D. Bernal and E. F. Carritt, Watts & Co., 1934.

Plekhanov, G. V., *Essays in the History of Materialism*, translated by Ralph Fox, John Lane, 1934.

Bukharin, N. I., and others, *Marxism and Modern Thought*, translated by Ralph Fox, Routledge and Kegan Paul, 1935.

Communism and a Changing Civilisation, John Lane, 1935.

Genghis Khan, John Lane, London, 1936 (reissued by Daimon Press, Castle Hedingham, 1962).

France Faces the Future, Lawrence and Wishart, 1936.

Portugal Now, Lawrence and Wishart, 1937.

The Novel and the People, Lawrence and Wishart, 1937 (reprinted by Cobbett Press with corrections and an Index; Preface by Mulk Raj Anand in 1944; new Preface by Jack Beeching in 1948).

This was their Youth, Secker and Warburg, 1937.

A number of writings on and by Ralph Fox are gathered together in *Ralph Fox: A Writer in Arms*, edited by John Lehmann, T. A. Jackson and C. Day Lewis, Lawrence and Wishart, 1937.

INDEX